MEN-AT-ARMS SERIES

EDITOR: MARTIN WINDROW

The Age of Charlemagne

Warfare in Western Europe 750-1000 AD

Text by DAVID NICOLLE Ph.D.

Colour plates by ANGUS McBRIDE

OSPREY PUBLISHING LONDON

Dedication
For Freddie

Published in 1984 by
Osprey Publishing Ltd
Member company of the George Philip Group
59 Grosvenor Street, London, W1X 9DA
© Copyright 1984 Osprey Publishing Ltd
Reprinted 1985 (twice), 1987, 1988, 1989

British Library Cataloguing in Publication Data

Nicolle, David
    The Age of Charlemagne.
    1. Military art and science—Europe—History
    2. Military history, Medieval
    I. Title   II. Series
    623'.094   U43.E95

ISBN 0-85045-042-X

Filmset in Great Britain
Printed in Hong Kong

Introduction

The Carolingian dynasty traced its origins back to a political alliance between Pepin of Landen (called 'the Old') and Bishop Arnulf of Metz in the first half of the 7th century. By that time effective power was already slipping out of the hands of the Merovingian kings of the Frankish state into those of Mayors. These latter were men who came to dominate the various palaces or power-centres in the loosely-knit Merovingian kingdom. Pepin of Landen was Mayor in Austrasia, the north-eastern heartland of the Frankish state. His daughter married Bishop Arnulf's son, and thus began the Arnulfing clan, which would later become known as the Carolingians.

A century later these Arnulfings were, in all but name, the rulers of the kingdom. From their power-base in Austrasia they controlled the army—or at least the best parts of it—and it was now rare for the titular Merovingian king even to have his own armed retainers. Charles Martel, victor of the battle of Poitiers over the Muslims in 732 AD, died in 741 AD; in time-honoured fashion, he had arranged for his authority to be divided between his sons, Carloman and Pepin 'the Short'. Apparently these brothers worked well together, and continued their father's policies and campaigns in harmony.

Charles Martel's wars had been largely defensive in purpose and conservative in character. Things were soon to change, however. In 747 AD Carloman decided to become a monk, and Pepin took over the whole kingdom. Thus, for the first time in many years, the Frankish state was unified. An Arnulfing now ruled the most powerful kingdom in western Europe. For three generations the Arnulfing clan had held barely disputed power. All that remained was for Pepin, as current head of the family, to depose the Merovingian king from his purely figurehead position.

This was still a momentous step to take. The Merovingian kings were mystical, almost semi-sacred figures whose family had its roots deep in the Franks' pagan past. The only way that Pepin could win a greater degree of divine sanction was by an even closer alliance with the Christian church. In 750 AD he won approval from Pope Zacharias to depose the last ineffectual Merovingian, and in the following year he had himself crowned in the great Abbey of St. Denis as king of the Franks. But whereas a Merovingian king was proclaimed by being raised on a shield in an echo of the family's distant origins as pagan Germanic war-leaders, Pepin was anointed with holy oil—a ceremony previously reserved for the most sacred Christian rituals of baptism and priestly ordination. In this way Pepin laid the foundations of an alliance

This gravestone of around 700 AD from the Magdeburg region shows the simple weaponry, sword, spear and shield, common to both Germans and Slavs in this frontier region. (Landesmuseum für Vorgeschichte, Halle)

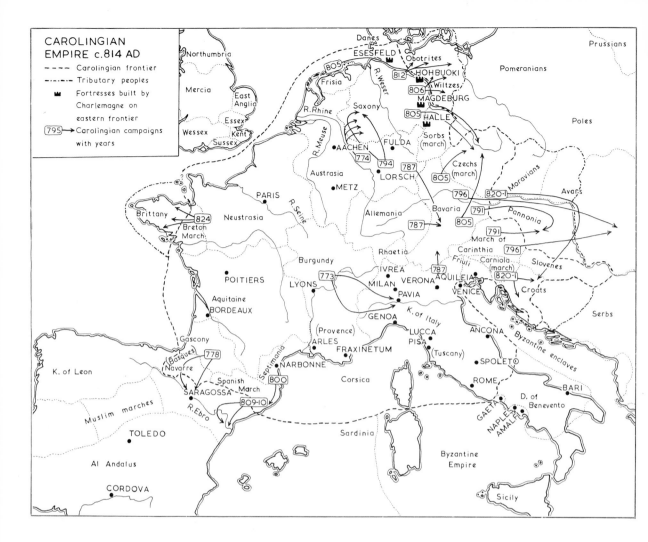

CAROLINGIAN
EMPIRE c.814 AD

- - - -   Carolingian frontier

-·-·-·   Tributary peoples

🏰   Fortresses built by
     Charlemagne on
     eastern frontier

795→   Carolingian campaigns
       with years

between the Arnulfing-Carolingians and the Church which was to prove extremely important in future years.

After 751 AD the nature of Pepin's campaigns also changed. Most were now aggressive, whether against pagans in the north, Muslims in the south or fellow Christians in Italy. While those against the Muslims in Septimania were the most striking aspect of Pepin's reign, his wars in Italy in support of the Pope would prove more important in the long run. It would also be wrong to see Pepin's campaigns against the Muslims as holy wars inspired by his new role as the Pope's champion. They were still primarily political campaigns, being directed against Arab rulers who had merely taken the place of previous Visigothic rulers against whom the Franks had warred for centuries. They were also closely linked to Pepin's internal campaigns in nearby Aquitaine, where the legitimacy of

Arnulfing rule was most persistently challenged.

In 754 AD a new Pope, Stephen III, actually came to France and, again at St. Denis, repeated Pepin's coronation. This time he also crowned Pepin's sons as fellow-kings, and declared them all to be Roman Patricians. This gave Pepin and his sons the duty to protect Rome and, in effect, to support the Pope against the Lombard kings who ruled most of Italy. Frankish expansionism was an almost inevitable result, and the unprovoked nature of Charlemagne's wars would follow an already well-established tradition.

Despite these far wider political and military horizons, and the broader ambitions which developed out of a close alliance with the Papacy, the Arnulfing-Carolingian clan still had to rely on its original power-base. This area, the foundation of both their material and their moral authority, lay between the rivers Rhine and Meuse. Today, though divided between France, Germany, Luxembourg, Belgium and the Netherlands, this region is at the heart of western Europe and contains much of the West's economic power. It had also been the Frankish homeland since the 4th century AD.

The Carolingian Dynasty

741	Death of Charles Martel, *Mayor* of the Merovingian kingdom.
741–7	Carloman and Pepin 'the Short' joint *Mayors*.
747–51	Pepin sole *Mayor*.
751–68	Pepin *King* of the Franks.
768–71	Charlemagne (Charles I) and Carloman joint *Kings*.
771–800	Charlemagne sole *King*.
800–14	Charlemagne *Emperor*.
814–40	Louis I, 'the Pious', *Emperor*.
840	Carolingian Empire divided between *Kings* recognising an overall *Emperor*.
840–55	Lothar I *Emperor*.
855–75	Louis II, 'the Young', *Emperor*.
875–77	Charles II, 'the Bald', *Emperor*.
877–81	Years of confusion.
881–7	Charles III, 'the Fat', *Emperor*.
887	Deposition of Charles III, and end of the nominal unity of the Carolingian Empire.

France

887	Duke Odo of Paris becomes effective ruler.
893–929	Charles, 'the Simple', nominal *King*.
929–36	Raoul of Burgundy, *King*.
936–54	Louis IV, 'of Outremer', *King*.
954–86	Lothair, *King*.
986–97	Louis V, 'the Coward', *King*.
997	End of Carolingian rule. Hugh Capet seizes the throne and becomes first Capetian *King* of France.

Germany and northern Italy

887–99	Arnulf, *King* and later *Emperor*.
891–4	Guy of Spoleto rival *Emperor* in Italy.
899–911	Louis IV, 'the Child', *Emperor*.
911	End of Carolingian rule in Germany and Italy.

919	Duke Henry of Saxony elected *Emperor*.
936–62	Otto I, 'the Great', *King* of Germany and subsequently *King* of Italy.
962	Otto I crowned *Emperor*.
973–83	Otto II *Emperor*.
983–1002	Otto III *King* and later *Emperor*.

The Carolingian Army 750-850 AD

Most historians agree that the Carolingian Age, from the 8th to 10th centuries AD, represented one of the most important turning points in European history. While this may have been less true of cultural history, it was certainly true of political and social history. The emergence of feudalism is only one example. It was probably even more true in the technological and military history of Europe, with the appearance of new farming and, to some extent, metal-working techniques. The adoption of the stirrup and subsequently of early versions of the high-framed war saddle, plus the pressure of rival and essentially non-western European cultures, combined to give birth to what are popularly regarded as medieval European styles of warfare. The most important 'non-western' rival cultures were, of course, the Arab-Iranian civilisation of Islam; the Asiatic Turco and Finno-Ugrian steppe cultures of the Avars, Bulgars and Magyars; and the archaic, though European, pagan culture of Viking Scandinavia.

Nevertheless, fundamental questions concerning Carolingian military organisation still remain unanswered. Reliable documentary sources are both few and inadequate, while the reliability of others is, for various reasons, highly suspect. It is clear, however, that within a quarter of a century the small and modestly trained army of Charles Martel had grown into a major war-weapon. Many scholars have tried to work out just how big Charlemagne's army was and, even more importantly, to decide what proportion was mounted and whether such horse-riding troops actually fought as cavalry. The resulting answers are almost as numerous as the scholars who produced them.

The *Isola Rizza Dish*. **This probably 6th-century Lombardic or Byzantine silver plate shows a warrior wearing lamellar armour and a plumed** *spangenhelm* **of obvious Central Asian inspiration. (Castelvecchio Museum, Verona)**

What might be said with some certainty is that early Carolingian military success was built on good leadership, adequate administration, and troops whose morale was almost consistently superb. It is also clear that the Carolingian army managed to adapt itself to face many and differing foes.

The Franks

The army of the early Arnulfings was a complex and by no means standardised organisation; nor did it show any major changes from 7th-century Merovingian forces. Evidence also indicates that the late 8th and early 9th centuries saw a further decrease in uniformity resulting from the sheer size of the Carolingian Empire as well as from its increasing internal divisions. This growing military force did, however, usually enjoy a greater political unity plus a marked superiority in both numbers and material over most of its foes. Under Louis 'the

Pious' early in the 9th century those élite forces directly under imperial control could even be ready to march within 12 hours of being called.

Charlemagne preferred all his free vassals to be warriors, but this was never entirely the case. All sections of society were, however, affected by the needs of war. This was particularly true of free men, who were liable for military service under the royal *bannum* or summons. General mobilisation, usually in a limited area in response to a specific crisis, was known as *lantweri*. This applied even to recently conquered peoples within a few years of their subjection. Yet it was on the Franks, the still largely German-speaking descendants of those tribesmen who had conquered Roman Gaul for the Merovingians, that military obligations fell hardest.

Professional warriors formed the personal followings of rulers and leading magnates. Previously referred to in Latin as *socii*, those loyal to the Mayor formed his *exercitus* (army) while those loyal to the magnates could combine to form an *exercitus generalis*. Such personal forces certainly dominated in Austrasia. Here the Palace warriors directly under royal control left their name in an entire region of modern Germany—the Palatinate, or Pfalz. The same was probably true in the western Frankish provinces of Neustria (northern France) and perhaps in conquered but still non-Frankish Burgundy. The situation in the thoroughly Romanised south of France was more complex. Other non-belligerent forms of obligation included *carnaticus*, or supplying the army with livestock for food; and *hostilense*, or the provision of carts and oxen.

Under the first Arnulfing kings and emperors the ruler's personal following formed a small standing army called the *scara*. Apart from being a hardened task-force of loyal troops, this *scara* also provided the leadership for other and perhaps less reliable warriors. When operating as distinct units, probably under *missi* imperial officers, this *scara* élite seems to have fought as close-packed armoured cavalry. The word ultimately came to refer to many such small military units. Charlemagne's *scara* consisted of young warriors living in or near the palace, perhaps in three ranks of seniority: the *scholares*, the *scola* and the *milites aulae regiae*.

Regional leadership originally fell to those *leudes*, or loyal subordinates, whom Charles Martel installed in areas which had resisted his authority and, more especially, along vulnerable frontiers. The existing organisation of the Church provided an administrative framework. By the mid-9th century the Counts, forming the senior level of secular authority, shared the government of areas called *pagii* with bishops and other top church leaders. As such they and the ecclesiastical authorities were responsible for summoning an army on receiving orders from the ruler. Their own personal followings were readily available, but the gathering of local levies is far less clear. Generally it seems that the Counts in turn instructed subordinates to list the *partants*, those who would actually join the army, and the *aidants*, those neighbours who would support the *partants*' families and farms while they were away. The quality and availability of local military equipment was also the direct responsibility of this regional leadership. Clearly, however, such a system was open to abuse, and the ruler had few means of checking on how local magnates carried out their responsibilities.

Failure to attend a general call to arms or *lantweri*

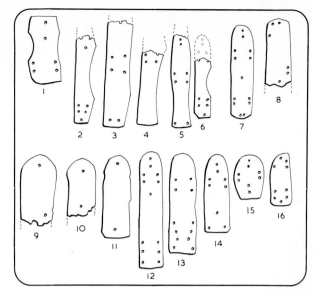

European and west Asian lamellar armours were very similar during the so-called Dark Ages: *1* Avar, 7–8 cent., from Kunszentmárton, Hungary; *2–6* Lombard, 7–8 cent., from Castel Trosino, Italy; *7* Viking, 800–950 AD, from Birka, Sweden; *8* Russian, 9–10 cent., from Khotomyet, Russia; *9–11* Khirgiz, 6–9 cent., from Turkestan; *12–16* Khirgiz, 9–12 cent., from Turkestan.

was punishable by death. Failure to obey the less critical *bannum* could, nevertheless, lead to a crippling fine called the *heribannum*, the size of which depended on an individual's wealth. The military manpower available to the early Carolingians was (according to Delbrück, Lot and Ganshof) around 5,000 men. Verbruggen puts his estimate at 2,500 to 3,000 horsemen plus 6,000 to 10,000 infantry. Werner reaches a total of 35,000 fully equipped horsemen plus up to 100,000 infantry and auxiliaries. What is clear is that only a fraction of the available total was ever used at any one time.

It is far less obvious whether or not these numerous Frankish horsemen fought as cavalry or more normally as mounted infantry. It now seems that cavalry were far from insignificant in Merovingian armies, despite misleading descriptions by cavalry-orientated Byzantine writers. It is even possible that the importance of Frankish cavalry had actually declined by the time of Charles Martel. Nevertheless, a small élite continued to fight on horseback with spears, while horses remained a particularly valuable item of booty. Mounted troops were used for raids, in ambushes or in pursuit, whereas real shock-cavalry charges were probably very rare. As such, late Merovingian and early Carolingian cavalry had a role directly paralleling that of early Muslim horsemen, but differing from those of Byzantine or Euro-Asiatic nomadic tribal cavalry. Frankish horsemanship was much admired, at least in western Europe. Late Roman horse-breeding estates, which had been inherited by the Merovingians and placed under the control of their *comes stabuli* (Constable), were now available to their successors.

It is also almost certain that early Carolingian cavalry made no use of stirrups even though their Avar and perhaps even some Lombard neighbours did so. There is no indication that Charlemagne's horsemen adopted the device, and no stirrups have been found in Frankish graves of the period. The young 'leapt' onto their horses' backs, as did the Muslim Arabs, while the aged used mounting steps. The question of Muslim stirrups is quite important in this context, as it has often been suggested that Arab pressure from Spain forced Carolingian armies to adopt cavalry warfare. Yet it is made quite clear in contemporary Arabic sources that, while Persians and Turks used metal stirrups, Arabs and in particular those of Al Andalus (Muslim Spain) did not—though some may have employed the primitive leather or rope 'loop stirrup'. The general adoption of stirrups, when it did occur somewhat later, resulted from Avar, Magyar or Viking pressure, not from that of the Arabs.

Even without stirrups a Carolingian horseman was well armoured and effective. The cost of his equipment, though it went down from 45 sous to 40 sous by the time of Charlemagne, was still very high. This meant that only the ruler and the regional leaders, secular or ecclesiastical, could afford to support armoured horsemen. In 792/3 AD a shield, lance, long and short swords were all required of a cavalryman, but not armour. By 805 AD things had changed, and if a man failed to wear a *brunia* body-armour he could lose both his status and the estates which accompanied it. This body-armour was, and remained, by far the most expensive single item of military equipment during the Carolingian era.

One important change that was taking place, and which may even have contributed to the adoption of heavier armour, was an increasing use of the sturdier Barb horse. Though it had been known in Europe during late Roman times the spread of this originally North African breed was greatly encouraged by the Muslim conquest of the Iberian peninsula.

The Carolingian adoption of horse-warfare may have been exaggerated; yet, by the time of Charles 'the Bald' later in the 9th century, all men who could afford a horse were specifically instructed to appear mounted. According to the *Annales Fuldenses* the Franks were no longer even used to fighting on foot by the year 891 AD. Yet the eventual acceptance of the stirrup did not mean an immediate development of the couched style of lance warfare. Such a style enabled a man to hold his weapon firmly beneath his armpit and thus deliver a more effective 'shock-cavalry' charge. Spears were still thrust with a swing of the hand, under- or over-arm, or by using both hands and no shield.

The role of Carolingian infantry is almost more obscure. The reappearance of massed infantry tactics in late Merovingian and early Carolingian times may merely reflect the fact that most warfare was now being fought in the eastern, less Romanised parts of the kingdom, which were traditionally poorer in horses. Warriors from backward Frankish societies east of the Rhine also seem to have been increasingly employed. Such troops clearly did not remain static and on the defensive but were capable of charges in the style of their pagan forbears. The obvious strategic role of rivers also points to the vital importance of infantry armies either transported by boats or whose baggage train went by river.

Finally there was the Carolingian commissariat. This was quite an impressive organisation, which would far surpass any other in Christian western Europe at least until the High Middle Ages. For the overland rather than riverine transport of baggage and siege equipment, leather-covered hooded ox-carts were used. These were apparently water-proofed so that they could be ferried across rivers. Lighter baggage was carried by pack-horses. Campaigns were planned long in advance, and local authorities along the proposed lines of march were instructed to collect supplies. Behind the troops marched another army, this time of merchants. Their toughness in defence of their baggage was acknowledged by all, but they were also widely accused of being drunken, lecherous, and prone to telling dirty jokes! The Carolingian army was, by contrast, a surprisingly sober and religious institution.

Equipment, Training and Morale

The cost of equipment ensured that only the richest could afford complete arms and armour. An élite of professional warriors was armed by its patrons while other men, including local levies, had to make do with whatever they could acquire. Some of the most powerful men in the state, like the *Domesticus* Dodo, could equip their followers with hauberks, helmets, shields, lances, swords, bows and arrows. At the other end of the scale, the duty of equipping those members of the levy who had to join an army was shared by those remaining at home.

The manufacture of weapons was still localised, but major centres of production were already emerging. The Rhineland was perhaps the most important, but it also seems possible that weapons manufacture had survived since Roman times in such northern Italian cities as Lucca and Pisa.

Long-distance trafficking in arms and armour was already worrying rulers and church leaders, because it included sales to pagans and Muslims. Most concern was expressed over deliveries to pagan Germans, Slavs and Danes. Exporting to Islam as yet attracted less condemnation and was, in any case, almost impossible to stop. Most trans-Mediterranean trade was still in the hands of Jewish merchants, and while Pisa had a flourishing commerce with Muslim North Africa and the East the survival of large Christian minorities in both these areas made trade contacts easier.

The basic character of western European military equipment had altered little since the fall of the Western Roman Empire. Any changes had generally resulted from Byzantine influence, and not until the 11th and 12th centuries would the transfer of fashions be in the opposite direction. The

The Porta San Paolo in Rome. In southern Europe such late Roman fortifications were rarely allowed to decay and served throughout the Carolingian era.

most famous and detailed description of a Frankish warrior is that of Charlemagne himself outside Pavia in 773 AD. As a monk of St. Gall put it: 'Thus appeared the Iron King with his crested iron helm (*ferrea galea christatus*), with sleeves of iron mail (*ferreis manicis armillatus*) on his arms, his broad chest protected by an iron byrnie (*ferrea torace tutatus*), an iron lance in his left hand, his right free to grasp his unconquered sword. His thighs were guarded with iron mail though other men were wont to leave them unprotected so that they might spring the more lightly upon their steeds. And his legs, like those of all his host, were protected by iron greaves (*ocreis*). His shield was of plain iron without device or colour.'

This is plainly an exaggerated and poetic description, particularly where the king's iron spear-head and the reinforcements or boss of his shield are concerned. It also portrays a man wearing a maximum of protection unavailable to the mass of soldiers. None the less, its basic elements reflect other sources such as the mid-8th century *Laws of the Ripuarian Franks*, which list helmet, *brunia*

A **Roman-style Carolingian fortress at Heisterburg Deister, Germany (after A. Tuulse).** *B* **Saxon-style Carolingian fortress at Pipinsburg, Germany (after A. Tuulse).**

body-armour, sword, scabbard, leg-defences, lance, shield and horse as the full equipment of a horseman. Their price totalled 44 *solidi*. A peasant's cow, by contrast, was worth 3 *solidi*. It is also worth noting that this 8th-century list is almost identical to that in an early 7th-century set of laws. Both probably referred to a horseman's ideal equipment, but a large proportion of Carolingian mounted men would have lacked helmet, armour or sword. Their equipment came to a mere 14 *solidi*, of which 12 were for the horse. The importance of unarmoured cavalry was, however, to decline rapidly during the 9th century.

Fewer sources describe infantry weaponry. Archery was important and would become more so, but as a larger proportion of the cavalry adopted armour so the effectiveness of infantry declined. In fact it would not even begin to be reversed until footsoldiers started using heavier weapons such as pikes and long-hafted Danish axes—in the late 10th and 11th centuries.

One question looms larger than any other where Carolingian armour is concerned. Did the *byrnie* or *brunia* ever consist of scales or was it simply a mail hauberk? Manuscript illuminations can be misleading, though some clearly show the insides of an

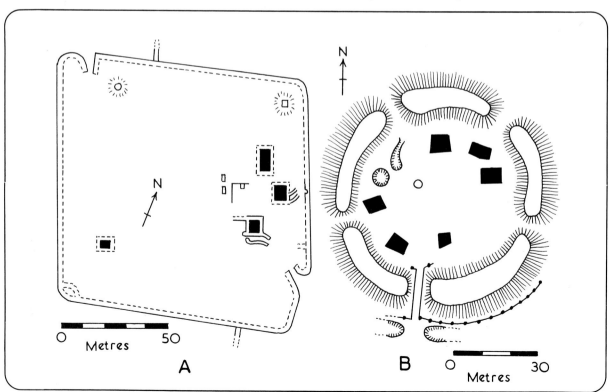

A

B

O Metres 50

O Metres 30

armour as being of a different colour, suggesting a scale construction of iron, bronze or horn on a leather or fabric base. The Germanic *brunia* was translated into Vulgate Latin as *torax* in the contemporary *Gloses de Reichenau*; and scale hauberks were certainly used by the Byzantines, to whom they were known as *thorakes* or *zaba*. Lamellar armour was also known in Italy, where it almost certainly reflected the Byzantine *klibanion*. By the 11th century, however, the terms *brunia* and *brogne* had become interchangeable with the mail *hauberk* or *haubert*. In early Scandinavian sources the *brynja* could be a heavy leather or felt coat without scales, while in later medieval Germany a *brunie* might be specifically reinforced with horn plates. That some scale armours persisted into the early 14th century is shown by indisputably accurate manuscript illustrations from widely separated parts of western Europe.

The question of the Carolingian coif or head and neck defence is almost as difficult. It could have been made of the same variety of materials as body armour. Yet it is believed to have appeared as a result of Avar influence, and Avars were in the Central Asian tradition which normally relied on an aventail suspended from the rim of a helmet. Mail coifs also seem to appear in early Christian and Jewish sources from Roman Italy and Syria. The segmented *spangenhelm* of ultimate Central Asian origin had predominated throughout western Europe since the barbarian invasions of the 4th and 5th centuries. Whether or not 'war hats' or *chapels de fer* of an essentially two-piece construction fastened to a comb and rim existed in Carolingian times is more debatable. Most authorities consider that their appearance in manuscripts is an artistic convention left over from late Roman times when this form of construction was widespread. On the other hand such 'war hats' would reappear in 11th/12th-century Scandinavia and in 12th-century Italy. Both areas were in close cultural, military or trading contact with Byzantium, where comparable helmets may have continued in use without a break.

References to arm and leg defences probably meant either long mail sleeves and long-skirted hauberks, or splinted iron vambraces and greaves of the type found in early medieval Scandinavian graves. Mail *chausses* to protect legs and thighs

One of the twenty-nine so-called Visigothic Towers of Carcassonne which were almost certainly added to the city's Roman defences in Visigothic, Merovingian or Carolingian times.

would later be adopted from the Magyars, along with the general use of stirrups. It would, of course, have been difficult and uncomfortable to ride without stirrups when the insides of one's legs were covered in armour.

Spears were the most common and cheapest weapons for all warriors. Those Frankish followers of King Carloman's envoy Dodo, who sacked the Lateran Palace in 769 AD, were seemingly only armed with spears, though they also wore mail. Such weapons for both horsemen and infantry had large horizontal lugs or wings beneath their blades. These were not to stop the weapon from penetrating too deeply into its victim, nor were they particularly suited to cavalry warfare as has sometimes been suggested. Lugs first appeared on 4th-century Germanic weapons, and probably indicated a parrying, almost fencing use of the spear. In other

A 9th-century French ivory plaque. The scale hauberk worn by this warrior has little in common with late Roman armour and may show a genuine type of Carolingian defence. (Bargello, Florence)

words the weapons were designed as pole-arms for both cut and thrust. Such a style of spear fighting is also indicated by the *languets* extending from the blade some way down the shaft. These clearly protected the wooden shaft from sideways cuts by an enemy, and were well known from the 7th century onwards. Neither lugs nor *languets* are relevant to the couched style of lance-play.

By Carolingian times the Frankish throwing axe or *fransiska* had been abandoned in favour of the *seax*, a single-edged short-sword or large dagger. This may again have been of nomadic Asiatic inspiration, as was the contemporary Islamic *khanjar*. While in Scandinavia the *seax* developed into a sizeable single-edged sword, in Frankish Europe it became a shorter dagger known as a *scramasax*.

The most expensive weapon was the sword. Its manufacture made the greatest demands on available technology, and it remained an essentially noble item of equipment. As true welding was unknown, rods of iron were twisted together, flattened, soft-soldered and then ground down. This so-called pattern-welding was not the same technique as that used in the 'damascened' blades of the Middle East, nor in the cast blades already being made in Central Asia. Some pattern-welded blades had harder, more carbonised metal at the centre than at their edges. In others the reverse was true; and in neither case is it certain that this was intentional. Nor is it confirmed that pattern-welded blades were stronger than those which were single-forged. It does, however, seem to have been easier for early medieval smiths to make good quality slag-free iron in small strips. A really fine sword with modest decoration probably took at least 200 man-hours to make, and its forging required from two to three hundredweights of charcoal. Small wonder that such costly weapons were kept rust-free in scabbards lined with oil-soaked fur or hair.

Carolingian archery saw more changes than most other forms of warfare. It was of major tactical importance on the eastern frontier in the first decade of the 9th century. Here Carolingian troops faced enemies either of Central Asian origin, or who had been influenced by Asiatic horse-archery techniques. Frankish horse-archers from the Abbey of Fulda are even mentioned, though such men were probably mounted infantry who dismounted to shoot and fight. In the 8th century Alemannic warriors used longbows of yew which were taller than a man. Such weapons were clearly for footsoldiers. Frankish settlers in Gaul had earlier adopted late Roman double-convex composite bows, but by the end of the 9th century these weapons had fallen out of use, except perhaps in Italy and southern France. They were replaced by short flat-bows of simple construction. Along with mounted archery the Carolingians may also have adopted the wood-framed saddle with a raised pommel from their Avar foes. The Byzantines certainly did so, though a general adoption of such saddles might have awaited the Magyar onslaught of the 10th century.

Finally there is the question of siege equipment; and here again the Avars had much to teach. In late

Merovingian and early Arnulfing times battering rams and assault ladders were the main means of reducing a fortress. The Avars introduced Chinese-style man-powered mangonels. These were soon adopted by the Byzantines and, in all probability, also came to form part of Charlemagne's siege-train. In 813 AD this was said to include a three months' reserve of supplies. It is also possible that the Franks learned of mangonels from Muslims in Spain and southern France.

The degree of training in a Carolingian army depended on the status of the warrior. All men knew how to use some weapon, as hunting was a part of everyday life. Children of the nobility would play with toy weapons and would be introduced to hard riding and hard living. From puberty they would train with javelin, bow and sword. *Milites*, or mounted warriors, also practiced with lances against a *quintaine* target or a dummy. Training as a unit involved war-games such as the *causa exercitii* in which equal forces, often from distinctive ethnic or tribal backgrounds, charged at each other, pretended to throw or wield their weapons, then turned in feigned flight with their shields protecting their backs. The opposing side would then repeat the performance, in a style of training exactly comparable to that seen in Byzantium and western Islam. Whether these manoeuvres grew out of early German tribal war-games or the *Marchfield* military reviews of the early 8th century is less clear.

Control on the battlefield was attempted by using signalling trumpets, which also helped maintain morale. Banners were mainly used as rallying points and to indicate the direction of attack, in which case they were in or ahead of the front rank. The importance of discipline was recognised, and Charlemagne seems to have regarded the ancient Roman army as an ideal. Certainly he insisted that no luxuries or superfluous finery be worn by his soldiers or their leaders.

The high morale of the Carolingian army resulted from its continued record of success and from the opportunities for personal advancement that it offered. Certainly there are instances of men choosing death if their leader fell. Ethnic or tribal solidarity contributed to this phenomenon. Paradoxically, Charlemagne endeavoured to downgrade the dukes of 'stem duchies', whose authority rested on tribal structures, by relegating them to

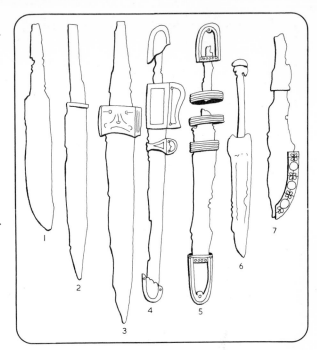

Daggers: *1–5* **Lombard, 7–8 cent., from Castel Trosino, Italy.** *6* **Moravian, 8 cent., from Mikulčice, Czechoslovakia;** *7* **Moravian, 9 cent., from Staré Mešto, Czechoslovakia.**

mere military leadership. Clearly he preferred the morale of his armies to be built on Christian solidarity. In many areas the Christianisation of his empire was, however, shallow or non-existent. Even in France the Franks had not been fully converted until well into the 8th century. Nevertheless, the military role of the clergy was fundamental. In Aquitaine some even trained in the use of the javelin; and whereas fighting men had to dress in a sober fashion, military churchmen relied on sumptuous robes and canopies to achieve their moral effect. After a battle they chanted Gradual Psalms for the fallen, gave the last rites, and helped the few doctors in an army-train to tend the wounded.

Offensive Strategy and Frontier Defence

Although Frankish wars took on an unprovoked expansionist character even under Pepin 'the Short', it was not until the time of Charlemagne that this was reflected in more ambitious strategy. Warfare was extremely frequent, and years without at least one campaign remained a rarity. The strategy employed by Carloman and Pepin was much like that of their father, Charles Martel. It was characterised by the seizure and garrisoning of fortified places in the Romanised south, and raiding for booty and tribute in the non-urbanised north and beyond the Frankish frontiers into Spain and Italy.

Charlemagne, by contrast, aimed for his enemy's heart. Political pressure sought to subvert the foe's military élite, and invasions headed for the enemy's capital or religious centre. Charlemagne's armies often attacked along two or more axes, making use of their habitual numerical superiority to force the foe to divide his forces or retreat in defence of his heartland. Speed and night marches were also characteristic of the best Carolingian armies.

While strategy might have become more ambitious, battlefield tactics remained essentially the same, although discipline and control probably improved. Mounted men acted in most cases as light cavalry skirmishers, making repeated charges with spears and javelins. Infantry were either attached to, or were closely associated with, such mounted units. Archery was primarily left to footsoldiers. A steady increase in the tactical importance of mounted troops led to a correspond-

The 10th-century castle of Castel Paterno in central Italy (after R. J. C. Jamieson): *A* **Plan;** *B* **Suggested reconstruction of wooden parapet.**

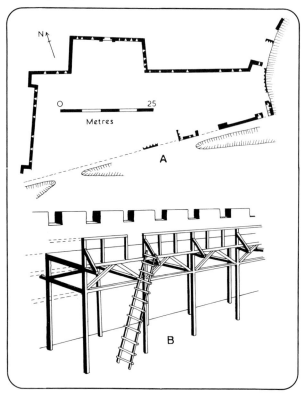

ing decline in the role of infantry until, by the end of the 9th century, Frankish wars were fought almost exclusively by cavalry. Sieges remained important, and here at least the cavalry had to dismount. Nevertheless the peasant, unfeudalised communities of the Frisian islands, the Dithmarschen region of northern Germany, the German Stedinger settlers along the river Weser and the highlanders of the Swiss heartland never adopted horse-warfare. Italian militia infantry did not die out either, and were to see a dramatic come-back in the late 10th or 11th centuries.

The Frankish cavalryman was, however, the typical warrior of 9th century western Europe. His *scara* was the most important unit or formation. In battle each *scara* apparently divided into several dense-packed *cunei*—cavalry formations of perhaps 50 to 100 men. Both *scara* and *cunei* had their own banners. Such units were able to make co-ordinated flank and rear attacks and to mount ambushes. There is even evidence of *ad hoc* uniforms being worn on certain occasions. The first mention of tactical reserves in Christian western Europe dates from the early 9th century, but these were not apparently a common tactical device.

The ruler normally led large armies in person but in his absence a *majordome* took charge. Franks almost always held the command of large formations, even those from other ethnic backgrounds. Military units, whose sizes varied considerably, were organised on a territorial basis under the local or regional leadership of a duke, marquis, count, bishop, abbot or other royal vassal. The number of such units required from each province was agreed beforehand in a survey or *indiculus*.

Important frontier defences were often garrisoned by élite *scara* units, but much less effort was put into maintaining and garrisoning fortifications in the Carolingian heartland. The main imperial palaces like that at Aachen were unfortified or had, at best, symbolic defences. Ingelheim was also open to the countryside. Smaller royal households called *curtes regiae* were sometimes fortified in a late Roman manner, and stood at certain strategic road junctions. They were normally square with rounded corners but no turrets, and were smaller than the Roman *limes* forts on which they were modelled.

In frontier regions, particularly in Germany, the situation was very different. Many Frankish citadels were linked with old tribal fortifications in the newly conquered regions of Saxony. West of the Weser River most were rectangular *curtes*, but to the east they were generally round, pallisaded earthworks like smaller versions of Saxon tribal forts. A rampart, moat and surrounding wall, as at Saalburg, were typical. At Heisterburg the main fortress was further protected by an irregularly shaped advance-post. Within such defences rough buildings were laid out almost at random. These fortresses were not, of course, designed as royal residences. A more sophisticated fort at Dorestat in Holland had three sections: a *curtes* to the rear, a *curticula* to the fore, and again an advance-post called the *pomerium*. In the middle was a rectangular house, the *sala regalis* for important visitors. All these defences acted both as administrative centres and as rallying points for troops. By contrast with pagan Slav or German areas further east, even Carolingian frontier 'marches' had few fortifications. Nor did these Carolingian defences use new building techniques; and most still employed the ancient Roman foot as their unit of measurement.

The special military organisation of frontier provinces called 'marches' was clearly more important than their fortification. Here the labour of local inhabitants could be summoned to construct or maintain defences. These were then manned by full-time local warriors called *wacta* or *warda* who were, in effect, military colonies organised into *scarae* or *excariti*. Such areas were governed by *markgrafen*, *margraves* or *marquises*. The best known, perhaps, was the Spanish March, an area including the Pyrenean mountains and their foothills which was to a large extent independent of Carolingian central authority. During the early years, in the late 8th and early 9th centuries, many renegade Arab and Berber warriors who had quarrelled with their own rulers played a major role in the defence of this newly created Spanish March. But generally, in what later became Catalonia and Aragon, defence rested on a levy of all free men. No real effort was made to seize territory from the Muslims, and warfare consisted of almost continual raid and counter-raid. To the south a comparable Muslim 'march' in the Ebro valley remained virtually independent of Cordova until the early

The 8th–9th century *Trier Apocalypse* includes some of the earliest representations of Carolingian warriors. It shows neither armour nor stirrups. (Cod. 31, f.63, Stadtbib., Trier)

10th century. By then, however, the Catalonian infantry levy had all but collapsed before a series of more determined Muslim attacks. Further west in Navarre defence continued to rely on local Basque infantry at least until the mid-10th century, and probably much longer.

Italy was another vital frontier zone for the Carolingians after their overthrow of the Lombard kingdom in 776 AD. In fact much of the peninsula consisted of defensive 'marches'. The first to be created was the March of Friuli facing the Slavs and Avars. Later came the March of Tuscany, which faced the Muslims based in Sardinia. To the south the Duchy of Spoleto eventually became an unofficial 'march' facing the Muslims of Sicily and southern Italy. Towards the end of the Carolingian era further 'marches' were created at Ivrea in western Lombardy, facing the Muslim base at Fraxinetum in Provence. Spoleto was also divided into two, and its eastern section around Ancona is still known as Marche to this day. Northern Dalmatia, on the other side of the Adriatic sea, acted as a further 'march' where, in 819 AD, a series of small forts were built as bases for mobile forces whose task was to harry the invading Slav Croats.

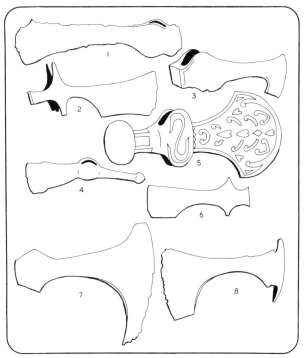

Axes: *1* **Avar, 7 cent. (?), from Csúny, Hungary;** *2* **Moravian, 8–9 cent., from Pohansko, Czechoslovakia;** *3* **Moravian, 8 cent., from Moravský-Ján, Czechoslovakia;** *4* **Magyar, 9–10 cent., from Kis-Dobra, Hungary;** *5* **Silver-decorated probable import from the Caucasus, 9 cent. (?), from Koŭrim, Czechoslovakia;** *6* **Polish, 10 cent., from Mazowsze Plockie, Poland;** *7–8* **Polish, 10–12 cent., from Lake Lednickie, Poland.**

At around the same time these Croats were tamed and converted to Christianity by missionaries from Aquileia. Comparable missionary centres supported frontier 'marches' in Germany, though not in Spain.

As might be expected, highly urbanised Italy saw some of the most ambitious Carolingian fortifications. Even so, they were crude compared to their Roman predecessors. Arrow-slits were few and towers rarely projected far enough to allow effective crossfire. Where possible, large ancient buildings were turned into fortresses. For example, Pope Leo IV converted the Tomb of Hadrian into what is still known as the Castel Sant'Angelo after the Muslim siege of Rome in 846 AD. Leo also extended the ancient fortifications of Rome to enclose the basilica of St. Peter, which had previously stood undefended outside the walls.

During the later Carolingian period the art of fortification advanced rapidly in Italy, with many ancient city walls being greatly strengthened with new towers. Even more striking was the number of small castles and village fortifications which sprang up across the country in the face of persistent Muslim and Magyar raids.

The art of castle-building developed more slowly beyond the Alps. Nevertheless, enough new and unofficial fortifications had been built by 864 AD for Charles 'the Bald' to issue his Edict of Pitres. This banned the construction of any more castles and ordered the destruction of the rest 'by 1st of August'. It seems unlikely to have been obeyed. More effective was another section of this Edict which ordered the construction of fortified wooden bridges across the Seine in an effort to halt Viking raids up-river. Paris itself was now merely a fortified island joined to the banks by two bridges with stone towers forming their landward gates. Viking raids were, in fact, to stimulate the next phase in the history of European fortification.

Allies and Subordinate Peoples

The Carolingian court was an exceptionally cosmopolitan one in its period of greatness. The same was true of the Carolingian army. One campaign, albeit an unsuccessful one, can be taken as an example: that against Saragossa in Spain in 778 AD. Apart from Austrasian eastern Frankish troops under Charlemagne's immediate control, Neustrian western Franks, Burgundians, Bavarians, Provençals, Goths from Septimania, Bretons and Lombards all took part as autonomous units.

It was in this campaign that Roland, governor of the Breton March, lost his life in a brutal skirmish immortalised in the later *Song of Roland*. Breton heavy cavalry were among the Carolingians' most effective non-Frankish troops. They still fought in a manner similar to those Alans who had been sent from the Caucasus to what was then Armorica by the late Romans, and would continue to do so until the 10th or even 12th centuries. Breton horsemen operated in densely packed but highly manoeuvrable groups using heavy spears, light javelins, swords and relatively heavy armour. Many of their horses were also armoured. Their tactics were comparable to those of the Magyars, though Bretons relied on javelins instead of arrows and thus approached their foes more closely.

To the south Aquitainians, Gascons and Provençals also retained their military traditions under both Merovingian and Carolingian rule.

Aquitainian city levies were responsible for garrisoning fortified places. Many, if not most, of the non-Frankish troops in Aquitaine were, however, Gascons of the *hostis Vascanorum* levy who, like their Basque cousins, fought primarily as infantry or light cavalry skirmishers using javelins. Gascons were renowned as mercenaries even in the 8th century. When they fought mounted their tactics consisted of repeated attack and feigned retreat. Provençals to the east remained thoroughly Romanised. Less information is available on their military traditions, but it seems likely that local *milites* fought in a late-Roman cavalry style while urban militias remained infantry primarily concerned with the defence of city walls.

The old Germanic kingdom of Burgundy seems to have adopted Roman military customs more readily than did the Franks or those Germans who conquered Italy. Gallo-Roman troops, some even retaining their unit identities, had been employed since the 5th century, and this tradition was inherited by the conquering Merovingians. Nobles even recruited slaves to train as soldiers as well as varied mercenaries, and the Burgundian army apparently soon consisted almost entirely of professionals. How far this was still true by Carolingian times is, however, another matter.

Another small Germanic kingdom to be incorporated into the Frankish Empire was that of the Bavarians, but its forces made no use of cavalry even under Charlemagne. By contrast the Goths of Septimania and the Spanish March, descendants of those Visigothic Germans who once ruled the Iberian peninsula, were renowned horsemen, relying on late Roman cavalry tactics of attack and feigned retreat. Prior to the conquest of Septimania by Pepin, these Goths actively helped the Muslims against their traditional Frankish foes. Nor was their Christian solidarity, like that of the Gascons and Aquitainians, helped by the fact that the Frankish reconquest of the south caused far greater damage than had the initial Arab and Berber occupation. But once it became clear that, like the Muslims, the Carolingians would allow the Goths

The ceremonial gateway of the Abbey of St. Nazarius at Lorsch was probably built around 774 AD. It is not genuinely fortified but is one of the few remaining buildings to reflect the capabilities of Charlemagne's military architects.

to retain their distinctive laws and customs, they became loyal allies—particularly against Gascon and Aquitainian rebels. Under Louis 'the Pious' a large proportion of Carolingian cavalry was concentrated in the Spanish March, and much may have been of Gothic origin.

Those dissident Muslims who also served in the Spanish March included cavalry relying on similar tactics. Many others, of course, were infantry. The Arabs, though probably not the Berbers, used much archery. Some were even horse-archers, fighting in Byzantine or Iranian fashion of shooting at rest or a slow walk rather than at a full gallop like Turks. Muslim mercenaries also fought in Provence in the mid-8th century.

While the military role of these subordinate peoples was important to the Carolingians, that of

Flags from mosaics and manuscripts: *1 Charlemagne receiving the Imperial Banner from St. Peter*, **9 cent. mosaic** (*in situ* **San Giovanni in Laterano, Rome**); *2–3 Psalterium Aureum* **from St. Gall, c. 880 AD (Cod. 22, ff. 144 and 140, Stiftsbib., St. Gallen, Switzerland);** *4 Psalter of St. Bertin*, **north French, c. 1000 AD (Ms. 20, f.29v, Bib. Munic., Boulogne);** *5 Beatus*, **Mozarab north Spanish, 10 cent. (Cathedral Lib., Seo de Urgel);** *6–7 Beatus* **from Tavera, Mozarab north Spanish, 975 AD (Cathedral Museum, Gerona).**

the Lombards was vital. Before Charlemagne overthrew the Lombardic kingdom in northern Italy, the Lombards had been building up personal military forces of retainers known as *gasindii*. These were among the best-equipped troops in Europe, with weapons, helmets, hauberks and *ocrea* leg-defences which reflected Avar influence. They were probably also particularly well trained, for they came to form the backbone not only of Carolingian armies in Italy but also of many invasion forces, such as that which destroyed the Avar state in 796 AD. At first Lombard military organisation remained unchanged. All free men had military obligations and provided their own equipment, this being assessed according to wealth. Horses were clearly more important in such Lombard forces than in Frankish ones, and many battles were fought predominantly by cavalry. Archery was, however, still an infantry affair, with at least some bows being of composite construction. The most important change following the Carolingian conquest was that military leadership now went to Franks who were, in turn, tightly controlled by royal *missi dominici* inspectors. Determined efforts were also made to curb the growth of private *gasindii* armies.

The gradual extension of feudal land tenure in return for military service during the Carolingian era was also seen in Italy, but here the lines of social stratification were already so blurred that it proved impossible for a truly feudal system to develop. By the time of Louis II an infantry levy system based on *aidants* and *partants* had spread to Italy, where a poor man might now be expected to serve as a coastguard. The poorest of all were, however, exempt.

Native Italians, normally referred to as 'Romans', had been brought back into the military system towards the end of the Lombard kingdom and were assessed on the same basis of wealth as the Lombards themselves. In those areas around Rome controlled by the Pope they had never, in fact, entirely lost their military role. An Italo-Roman militia played a major role in various regions—including Rome—under real or nominal Byzantine authority, and was organised along Byzantine lines. The Italo-Roman nobility of the area around Rome also formed a small but effective army, so much so that the Roman clergy found it necessary to use their growing economic power and wealth to recruit a balancing force of assorted mercenaries. By this time, however, no trace of ancient Roman military organisation remained. Certain ceremonial survivals, such as the silk caparisons worn by horses in prestige parades, were probably less a Roman inheritance than an adoption from Byzantium.

The Avars also made a major contribution to Carolingian military might. This lay not in their role as a subordinate people following their defeat, though this was locally significant, but rather in the new ideas and forms of military organisation that they brought to Europe. Many were adopted during Carolingian wars against these Asiatic invaders, but more were probably learned from the Avars after their ruin. Their proverbial wealth and that of their semi-mobile capital was not based solely on loot for, like many nomadic peoples of the steppes, the Avars were skilled metalworkers and maintained wide trading contacts. Their capital entered European history and legend as The Ring, a ninefold rampart of clay and stone topped by hedges and pallisades without gates. In reality The Ring probably referred to a series of sophisticated earthworks surrounding the Avar state. Certainly the Avars introduced more advanced siege engineering of Chinese origin into Europe. Though normally fighting with lances and Chinese-style bows and using cast-iron stirrups and felt or lamellar horse-armour, their armoured cavalry seemed more prepared to fight on foot than other steppe peoples. Perhaps this again reflected a strong Chinese element in their culture. They were, in fact, probably descended from the defeated Turkish Juan-Juan people of 5th-century Chinese sources. Even their name, Avars, means 'exiles' in early Turkish.

By contrast the Saxons, who were the Carolingians' other most determined foes, had almost nothing to offer in terms of military technology. Their tribal society, in four classes of nobles, freemen, bondsmen and slaves, was comparable to that of the early Franks and Anglo-Saxons. Like the Christian Franks living east of the Rhine, these pagan Saxons wore little armour and fought with spear, sword and axe. Though horse-raising was one of their main trades they fought almost exclusively as infantry. After their final submission

The *Stuttgart Psalter* of c. 825 AD again includes no stirrups and most armour seems to be of scale construction. (Cod.2°.23f, f.21v, Stuttgart Landesbib.)

to Charlemagne in 785 AD the Saxons became liable for military service, and took part in campaigns against their Slav neighbours within four years. Early in the 9th century many Saxon warriors were recorded using bows and half a century later most were still clearly unarmoured infantry.

Finally there were the Slavs. Various northern tribes became Carolingian clients or vassals in the 9th century even though the bulk of their people remained pagan. The Obotrites of the Baltic coast were, in fact, victims of the first serious Viking attack when Danes raided their area in 808 AD. Most of these northern Slavs fought on foot with spears, shields and simple bows. Only their leaders were mounted; but there is no evidence that they were poorer in equipment than their German neighbours. Although swords were imported from the north and west other gear was manufactured locally, and by the 10th century Islamic geographers could write of wealthy iron-working centres in the northern Slav region. From the mid-10th century the warriors of such areas were barely distinguishable from the Carolingians except, perhaps, for a few eastern influences in their equipment and their use of light, long-hafted war-axes. Among those who remained pagan short or shaven hair was the rule, only the high-priest of the idol Svantovit at the Arkona shrine being permitted to wear his uncut.

Various southern Slav tribes in what is now

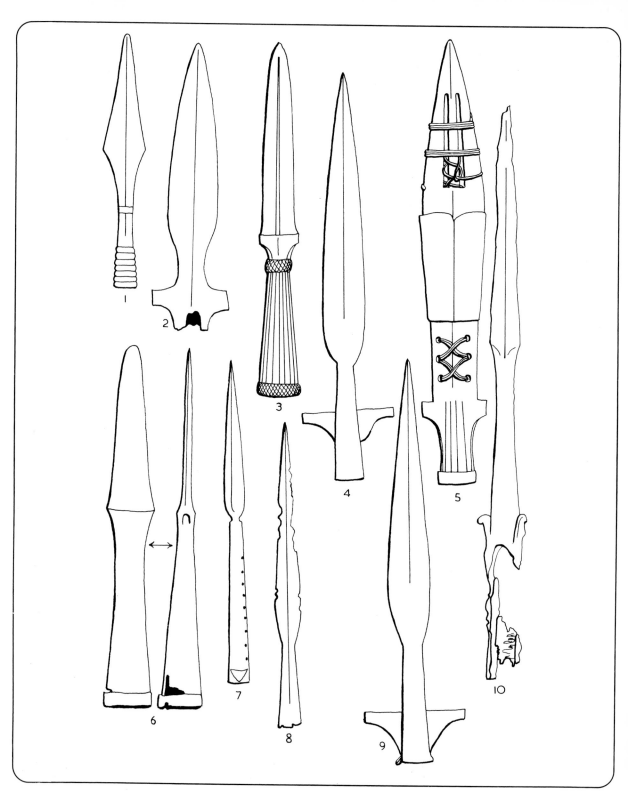

Spearheads in the western and eastern traditions: *1* Moravian, 8 cent., from Moravský-Ján, Czechoslovakia; *2* Magyar, probably captured from the Germans, 9–10 cent., from Keczöl, Hungary; *3* Magyar, 10 cent., from Esztergom, Hungary; *4* Polish, 10 cent., from Pomorze, Poland; *5 Spear of St. Maurice* **given by Emperor Otto III to King Boleslav of Poland in 1000 AD,** German; *6* Magyar, 10–11 cent., from Pécs-Üszog, Hungary; *7* Northern Slav (Wiltzes or Obotrites), from Szczecin, 10 cent., Poland; *8* Polish, 10–11 cent., from Lake Lednickie, Poland; *9* Polish, 10 cent., from Wielkopolska, Poland; *10* Lombard, 8 cent. (?), from Castel Trosino, Italy.

Austria and Yugoslavia were also either conquered by the Carolingians or forced into a vassal status. Though their military traditions had naturally been influenced by Byzantium, their swords seem largely to have been imported Merovingian and Carolingian types. The *miles ensifer* warriors of what is now Slovenia and even Croatia would, in fact, soon become virtually indistinguishable from the troops of western Europe. Spears and shields were the most common weapons and most men fought on foot. Slings and short swords comparable to the Germanic *seax* are also mentioned. The curved Asiatic sabre had even less influence among these southern Slavs than among their northern cousins, though it would have a profound impact among the eastern Slavs. Narrow-bladed axes may have been adopted before the 8th century in Croatia, while in Byzantine-influenced Serbia bows became the favoured weapons. Scale or lamellar armour of apparently Byzantine inspiration was also common in Serbia and must surely have influenced Croatia to the west. Western-style mail was, however, apparently preferred by those few Croatian and Slovenian warriors who could afford it.

The Failure of the Carolingian System 850-950 AD

Of all the dangers that threatened Christian western Europe in the 9th and 10th centuries, that from the Vikings was the most serious. Persistent raiding started in the mid-9th century, with the rich merchant communities of Frisia as a first target. Thereafter France was worst hit, with Germany escaping relatively lightly. Charles 'the Simple's' acceptance of a Viking province along the lower Seine, soon to become known as Normandy, was merely a recognition of reality—though Charles also hoped to use these Scandinavian settlers as a buffer against further Viking invasions.

The main reason for the Carolingian failure to defeat the Vikings was a collapse of central authority. This really began on the death of Louis 'the Pious' in 840 AD. The Empire was then divided between his sons; and although one assumed the title of Emperor his authority over his brother kings

was little more than a façade. The reality was more often one of Carolingian civil war while the Vikings ravaged unchecked. In Aquitaine a non-Carolingian aristocrat even tried to win independence, perhaps despairing of effective Carolingian help against the raiders. In 887 AD, with the death of Charles 'the Fat', even the nominal unity of the Empire came to an end.

On a military level the Viking raids succeeded because the Carolingian system had been designed primarily for attack, not for defence. Military organisation had started to crumble almost as soon as the state ceased to expand, to win booty and to acquire land with which to reward its soldiers. Henceforth the ruler was weakened by a need to use his own treasure and royal estates to maintain his followers' loyalty. Many defensive 'marches' also deteriorated during the first half of the 9th century,

A late 10th-century south German ivory book-cover showing the spear and shield which remained the basic equipment of most early medieval warriors. (V & A Museum, no. 380–1871, London)

particularly those in Brittany, along the Danish frontier, in Spain, the Balkans and the Mediterranean islands. Elsewhere poor but free men had generally lost their military role and instead merely paid taxes to support a small élite of armoured cavalry. The resulting lack of good infantry greatly hindered local defence. Where they did survive, as in Saxony, their numbers were usually enough to defeat the Vikings. Elsewhere attempts to mobilise untrained peasants often led to their being massacred.

There is no real evidence that Scandinavian military equipment was superior to that of their foes. Much, in fact, had been imported from the Carolingian Empire. The Vikings did, however, enjoy the advantage of strategic surprise by raiding from the sea and up rivers. They also fought with an awe-inspiring pagan ferocity. The Vikings also seem to have made greater use of infantry archery. Simple longbows were a common weapon, although composite bows—using various layers of glued wood rather than horn and sinew—were known. Viking base-camps of earth and timber were also very advanced, perhaps having been learned from the numerous *grody* forts of Slav north-eastern Europe. Most were built on islands or beside rivers. For their part the Christians hurriedly rebuilt their *castella* and *castra* defences, city walls and fortified monasteries, particularly in the central region between the Loire and Rhine. A resulting increase in siege warfare saw Carolingian cavalry often fighting on foot, both in attack and defence. Paradoxically, when the Vikings started to adopt horse-warfare in the late 9th century they could generally be defeated by the Carolingians.

While the top ranks of French regional leadership

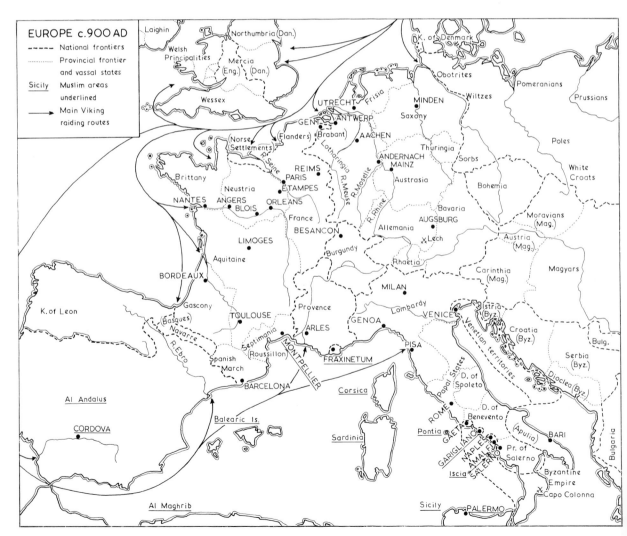

tended to flee the Viking threat, since there was no profit in resistance, those at a lower level had to remain. Their defence, though static, was more effective than is generally realised. Later, however, there was a growing tendency to bribe the raiders to go elsewhere. A similar state of affairs developed in Germany in the late 9th century, with the higher aristocracy fleeing to cities, castles, forests or marshes. Large ecclesiastical landowners could call upon both noble and peasant levies in their defence, but were rarely able to muster their full strength. Meanwhile Emperor Henry I also normally paid bribes to the Vikings; but he used the time so won to re-organise his armies, recruit more of the heavy cavalry who had earlier proved themselves against the pagan Slavs, and strengthen his fortifications. He also enlisted that Saxon peasantry who had military experience in border wars with their Slav neighbours, plus mercenary units of former outlaws. These men then garrisoned the new fortifications. By contrast, few comparable improvements were seen in France.

The second threat to menace Europe in the 9th and 10th centuries came not from barbarians but from a rival civilisation which was, in most respects, more advanced than that of the Carolingian Empire. The Saracens, as Muslim Arabs and Berbers were known in the West, had first assaulted Europe in the 8th century. Their threat had petered out, however, partly as a result of early Carolingian resistance, but mostly because the Islamic conquerors had over-extended their lines of communication and their available military manpower. The collapse of the Umayyad Caliphate in 750 AD and the regional fragmentation of western Islam that rapidly followed then gave Mediterranean Christendom a century of relative peace.

In 800 AD, the year that Charlemagne was crowned Emperor, the Aghlabid dynasty won independence in Tunisia. It was from here that the greatest Saracen threat to western Europe would soon come. This revival of Muslim pressure resulted mainly from a Byzantine naval decline early in the 9th century, Byzantium having been the dominant maritime power until then. Muslim Spain joined in this new offensive, though on a small scale, with raids against southern France and Italy. The whole western part of the Muslim world was, of course, now enjoying a great economic and cultural revival.

Most raids were apparently undertaken by volunteers rather than regular armies, but even so Islam won effective control of the western Mediterranean from 827 to 960 AD.

The scale of some attacks was astonishing. In 846 AD, for example, 11,000 men with 500 horses and 73 ships attacked Ostia and Rome—this was in fact a proper Aghlabid army rather than a group of adventurers. In many respects the Saracens' equipment was also superior to that of the Carolingians. Their advanced siege engines were the same as those of the Muslim east. By the mid-9th century they used *naft* or Greek Fire at sea, making

Arms and armour in metalwork and manuscripts: *1* **Lombard ornamental belt-end, early 8 cent. (?), from Castel Trosino, Italy;** *2* **'Saul' in** *Psalterium Aureum* **from St. Gall, c. 880 AD (Cod.22, Stifsbib., St. Gallen, Switzerland);** *3* *Psalter,* **north French, 9 cent. (Bib. Munic., Amiens);** *4 Apocalypse,* **probably Spanish, c. 840 AD (Ms.99, Bib. Munic., Valenciennes).**

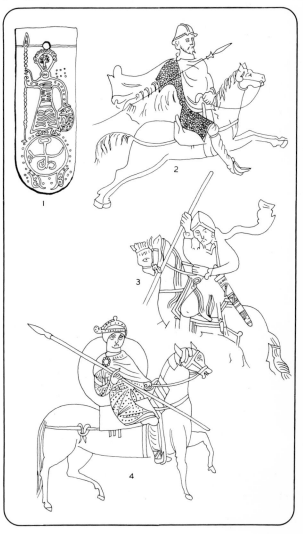

even greater use of it in the 10th century. Their bows were of a particularly large composite type developed from the old Romano-Syrian weapon. Saracen tactics were similarly sophisticated, with a habitual use not only of reserves but of hidden reserves in pre-arranged ambush positions. Small wonder that the anonymous writer of the *Salerno Chronicle* described them as the 'most astute nation of Arabs' who, 'as they are cunning by nature, and more forward-looking in evil than others, examined the fortifications of the place [here referring to Bari] more minutely and made their way into the city by hidden places at night-time. . . .'

Despite the all-too-frequent failure of the Carolingians to support the Italians, Lombards and local Franks, the Christians had the advantage of numbers and a similarly booming economy. Largely alone, though with occasional aid from Byzantium, they managed to defeat the first wave of Saracen attacks by 870 AD. But within a few years the raids began again just as ferociously. This time the Muslims established fortified bases in Europe. Of these the most dangerous were those at the mouth of the Garigliano River in Italy and at Fraxinetum in Provence. The former was destroyed in 915 AD, but the latter survived until 972 AD. Much of Apulia was occupied for most of the second

half of the 9th century, while Sicily and Sardinia remained under Muslim control until the 11th century.

The nominally Byzantine but effectively independent Italian city of Naples maintained an alliance with these Muslims throughout much of the 9th and 10th centuries. So, to a lesser degree, did Salerno. The Saracens who seized control of Provençal Fraxinetum were originally invited in by one side in a civil war, and an even greater variety of local Italian and southern French rulers employed Muslim mercenaries from Libya, Crete, Spain and Sicily. Many settled, though their integration into Christian civilisation was very gradual. The main Saracen attempt to colonise Italy by force of arms was defeated when their fortified base on the Garigliano was overrun. Despite all the disruption caused by these events, Italy enjoyed steady economic, agricultural and trading growth in the 9th and 10th centuries, a fact which was to have a profound effect on the whole course of European history.

The third threat to face Carolingian Europe in the 10th century was the last in the line of invasions and settlements by nomadic steppe-peoples which had begun with the Huns in the 4th–5th centuries. (The Mongols of the 13th century were in a different category, as they made no effort to colonise western Europe.)

The Magyars were an amalgamation of various Finno-Ugrian and Turkish tribes who, driven from their lands in southern Russia and apparently losing most of their womenfolk in the process, conquered and settled what is now known as Hungary in the last years of the 9th century. Though their culture was nomadic, the Magyars were by no means barbarians. Some were probably Christian, others were Jews. Their aristocracy was essentially Turkish and their art, their craftsmanship and above all their weaponry were superb. The Magyars, despite their misfortunes and migrations, kept in close trading contact not only with Byzantium but also with the sophisticated eastern provinces of Islam. It has, in fact, been suggested that the Magyar aristocracy was at this period culturally akin to that of Islamic Iran—though not, of course, being Muslim.

Each of the 180 Magyar tribes was led by a *hadnagy* or duke. These men in turn elected their

A 9th-century French *Psalter* showing an unarmoured warrior wearing either a *spangenhelm* or perhaps a fluted helmet. (Ms.18, f.67, Bib. Munic., Amiens)

c. 750-800:
1: Gascon cavalryman
2: Austrasian 'scara' mounted infantryman
3: Lombard 'gasindius' cavalryman

A

c. 800-850, Frankish heartland:
1: Carolingian 'scola' heavy cavalryman
2: Armorican cavalryman
3: Frankish infantry levy

B

c. 800–850, northern and eastern frontiers:
1: Avar horseman   2: Western Slav tribesman   3: Saxon infantry levy

C

c. 800-850, southern and western frontiers:
1: The Emperor Charlemagne
2: Papal guardsman
3: Mounted infantryman, Spanish March

D

c. 850-950, the Viking threat:
1: French cavalryman, c. 900
2: French local infantryman, early 10th C.
3: Carolingian nobleman, late 9th C.

E

c. 875-975, southern France and Italy:
1: Italian infantry levy, early 10th C.
2: Italian 'gastald' cavalryman, early 10th C.
3: North African infantry archer, early 10th C.

F

c. 900–950, the Magyar threat:
1: German infantryman, first half 10th C.
2: German cavalryman, first half 10th C.
3: Magyar cavalryman, first half 10th C.

c. 950-1000:
1: Southern French knight, late 10th C.
2: Lotharingian knight, late 10th C.
3: Western Slav rebel, second half 10th C.

prince, who had to be of the ruling Arpad family. Major decisions of peace or war were decided by the people in assembly, as in early pagan Scandinavia. Their foes regarded them as particularly well disciplined in battle and, according to the *Chronica Hungarorum*, the Magyar army was divided into seven sections of related tribes. These in turn consisted of units of hundreds and dozens. Warfare, and above all raiding, was the preserve of the warrior aristocracy. The mass of the people, both conquered Slavs and Magyars, had settled down as peasant farmers or herdsmen by the end of the 10th century.

One of the main reasons for raiding seems to have been to capture women, which lends credence to the story that the Magyars' families were mostly seized by their foes when the tribes fled southern Russia. It was the speed of these summer raids and the enormous distances covered that astonished their western European foes. In camp the Magyars made field fortifications with their waggons. In battle they fought in the typical manner of steppe nomads, relying on horse-archery, sudden attacks and feigned retreats. They rarely assaulted fortified places, preferring to impose a blockade. They also maintained contact between their raiding groups by means of smoke-signals.

Once established on the Hungarian plain the Magyars made no further attempts to conquer territory though they did impose tribute where they could. They also used their defeated Slav neighbours' lands as bases from which to raid further. This was all part of the Magyars' strategy of creating a depopulated or at least impoverished defensive zone around their own newly won country. They naturally saw the Bavarians to the west as the greatest threat, particularly as this German province still claimed authority over the old Carolingian March in western Hungary. On the other hand many Christian rulers, German and Italian, were happy to make short-term alliances with the Magyars during those civil wars which brought the Carolingian Empire to an end. The Magyars' campaigns differed from those of these neighbours only in their speed and the distances covered. The cumbersome late Carolingian armies did, however, enjoy some advantages: in particular, their heavier armour, weapons and horses, and the fact that rain often hampered Magyar archery.

The bow was the Magyar's most effective weapon. This was of a composite type similar to the earlier Hun bow and much straighter in outline than that of the Magyars' Avar predecessors. Compared to their late Carolingian enemies the Magyars possessed very little armour. As was normal in such nomadic tribal societies only an aristocratic élite wore metal armour, the rest relying on heavy felt coats and perhaps leather lamellar protection. On the other hand this aristocratic armour was of particularly fine quality, according to Russian, Byzantine and Islamic sources. Magyar lamellar almost certainly influenced that of Scandinavia and probably that of the eastern Slavs as well. Shields rarely seem to have been used.

An ivory situla from Milan c. 980 AD. The mailed warriors wear helmets with apparent combs or ridges along the crown. (V & A Museum, n.A.18–1933, London)

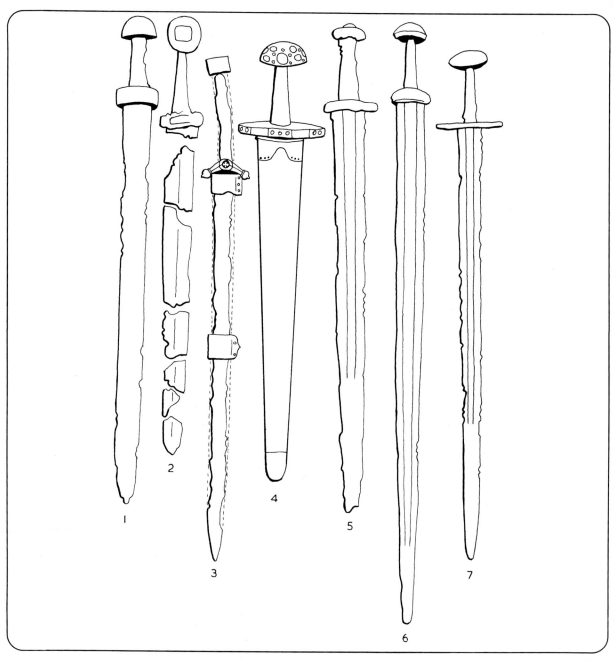

Swords: *1* **Moravian, 8 cent. (?), from Dolné-Krškany, Czechoslovakia; *2* Late Avar or early Magyar, 9 cent., from Gáva, Hungary; *3* Magyar, 10–11 cent., from Nemes Ócsa, Hungary; *4* German (with scabbard), late 10–early 11 cent. (Essen Minster Treasury); *5* Polish or German-import, 10 cent., from Kacice; *6* Polish or German-import, 10 cent., from Machów, Poland; *7* German-import, 10–11 cent., from Ostrow Lednicki, Poland.**

Other standard Magyar weapons were a light spear; sometimes a mace (which suggests that helmets were not as uncommon as was thought); and a typically Central Asian curved sabre. This was known to the Christians as a *gladius hunniscus* or

Hunnish sword. Magyar sabres were characterised by curved hilts and down-turned quillons. By the mid-10th century the Magyars were also clearly using siege-engines.

The Carolingian Empire had a foretaste of what the Magyars could do when Bulgar raiding forces penetrated their eastern frontiers earlier in the 9th century. The Bulgars were also originally a nomadic steppe people, but they certainly never matched the 30 or so major raids deep in Italy, Germany, Burgundy, France and even Aquitaine that the Magyars achieved between 898 and 955 AD. Nevertheless, only the eastern provinces of Bavaria, Thuringia and Saxony were ever in danger of extinction. Even these areas survived; but the political fragmentation of early 10th-century Germany was a direct result of Magyar pressure. So was the rise of a new dynasty—that of the Saxon Ottonians, which would inherit and to some degree reunite Carolingian Germany.

The Revival of Europe
950-1000 AD

The second half of the 10th century saw relatively few changes in European arms and armour, but some important developments in social and military organisation. It was at this time that medieval feudal Europe rose from the ashes of the Carolingian Empire. The Viking, Saracen and Magyar threats had been contained. Christianity was advancing, often at the point of a sword, in Poland, Hungary, Scandinavia, Spain and the Mediterranean islands. Economic expansion financed the building of new state structures, and this was nowhere more obvious than in Germany under its new Saxon Emperors. Here the revived power of old pre-Carolingian tribal duchies was reflected in the regional organisation of large armies, particularly around Saxony.

The Saxon *exercitus* army was, in fact, fundamental to the power of Henry I and the Ottos who succeeded him. These new Saxon rulers encouraged the breeding of many more horses so as to enlarge the cavalry element in their forces. There was also a great increase in the manufacture of arms—and above all, swords—in Saxony. Nevertheless, power in Ottonian Germany was far more fragmented than under the Carolingians. By the end of the 10th century armies were dominated by contingents of *milites* or vassals under counts and margraves whose loyalty could not always be relied upon.

A typical such army is described in a unique surviving manuscript. This *Indiculus Loricatorum* of 981 AD lists the 2,090 armoured cavalry owed by certain major secular and ecclesiastical landholders in western and southern Germany. From these was selected the army which was to be defeated by the Muslims of Sicily at Capo Colonna in 982 AD. Three-quarters came from church estates, the rest from secular lords. The largest church contingent totalled 100 men, 40 was the largest from a lay lord. The smallest totalled ten men. To these had to be added the Emperor's own troops, including a bodyguard recruited from specially trained slaves. Such guards developed into the serf-cavalry *dienstleute* (Latin *ministeriales*), who were to become characteristic of medieval Germany. The local warriors or *agrarii milites* were divided into groups of nine, one of whom always had to be serving with the garrison of a fortified place while the rest looked after his land. Earlier in the 10th century many such men were still infantry. The élite of all troops was, however, the armoured cavalryman, *miles armatus*. The rest were called simply shield-bearers, *clipeati milites* or *scutiferi*.

Fighting in close-packed formations of perhaps 50 men, such cavalry dominated later 10th-century warfare, and were particularly effective against the Slavs. Their training included 'games' which, based on those of Carolingian times, were the ancestors of the medieval tournament. Each unit had its own banner. Flags were now a highly developed form of recognition signal. Otto I's élite unit of cavalry had one portraying the Archangel Michael, while the German Emperor's own banner was later recorded as consisting of a silken dragon on a pole surmounted by an eagle, the whole being mounted in a four-horse cart similar to an Italian city's *carroccio*.

Imperial control of the eastern frontier provinces was stricter than elsewhere. A network of fortified *burgwards* was created. These were garrisoned and maintained by a mixture of conquered Slavs and the new German settlers. Local counts were forbidden to force any man to do such duties outside his immediate home area however. Slav vassal states beyond the frontier also contributed troops to Imperial armies. Poland and Bohemia, for example, normally sent 300 men each.

Throughout this period the importance of infantry and unarmoured cavalry declined sharply, though unarmoured Saxon horsemen still proved very effective in guerilla warfare against continuing Viking raids. Free peasants had now been virtually excluded from the armies, except as despised auxiliaries, while urban militias did little more than defend their city walls. With the increasing number of castles, even such fortified towns were of limited military importance. In Austria the Margrave summoned cowherds and swineherds against the Bohemians only in direst emergency. Yet, despite this general decline, there was already some evidence of a rise in the status of certain infantry forces. The cities of Flanders and Brabant were one example, and their infantry pikemen were later to become among the most sought-after mercenaries in western Europe.

The process of political disintegration was even more pronounced in France. Local defence led by local lords had proved the only way of dealing with Viking raids, and by the mid-10th century the last Carolingian kings had no real power. Many of the rising regional dynasties did not come from the old Carolingian aristocracy. They, their castles and their *mesnies*—extended families linked by mutual interest and feudal support—were a thrusting new element in French society. Unfortunately their belligerent way of life led to almost endless small-scale local conflict, particularly after the Viking threat had disappeared. Rulers were drawn into this petty warfare as they tried to assert a vanished authority in brief campaigns, mostly of siege warfare, which involved very small forces.

Fragmentation of authority was increasingly obvious the further one travelled from Paris, and was worst of all in the south. Here even the regionally unifying factors of feudalism were barely felt. Many families owned a single castle and accepted the overlordship of none but a distant and powerless king. Beyond the Pyrenees, in those provinces of Catalonia and Aragon which had grown out of Charlemagne's Spanish March, an upsurge of Muslim power in the neighbouring Ebro valley virtually wiped out French influence from 950 to 985 AD. When Hugh Capet, Duke of Paris, seized power in 987 AD, northern France seemingly lost interest in its nominal possessions south of the Pyrenees. But, in a strange reversal of roles, these same areas continued to have a close military interest in southern France.

During this essentially feudal period of French history armoured cavalry totally dominated warfare and it seems clear that, in the north at least, the *milites* were always mounted *equites*. It is also worth noting that heavily armoured Bretons were still regarded as excellent cavalry. North of the Loire most *milites* were knights of the minor aristocracy, but non-noble cavalry also played a role. Many were mercenaries and all were equipped by their lords or paymasters. In southern France, Provence, Catalonia and Aragon a whole new class of professional *milites*, many of servile origin, grew up in the late 10th century. Unlike those of northern France they were almost all soldiers of fortune, and included both infantry and cavalry. Some are recorded serving the Muslim rulers of Spain where many converted to Islam, and they may even have fought in North Africa.

Though the northern French *miles* was primarily an armoured cavalryman he could also fight on foot, particularly in siege warfare, and consistently proved superior to that levy of peasants who were still occasionally called upon to serve as infantry. In the deep south, however, in Navarre and the Basque mountains, infantry continued to dominate. The javelinmen of these areas were again to be sought after as mercenaries in the 12th century.

Despite the collapse of the Carolingian military system much Frankish terminology survived. The élite warrior *scara* became the German, French and Italian *scharen*, *echielles* and *schieri*; the *bandwa* ensign became the *banieren* and *bannières*; the *roi* measure of troops the *conroten* and *conrois*. An ancient Germanic term probably also lay behind the *bataelgen*, *batailles* and *battaglie* battalions. The same was true of many items of arms and armour.

While in Germany an Ottonian dynasty of Saxon origin inherited power from the last feeble Carolingians, France had to wait until 997 AD before Hugh Capet, Duke of Paris and effectively already ruler, was formally crowned king. From him was descended a vigorous new dynasty, but these Capetians took over a desperately feeble power-base. Only the regions immediately around Paris, Orleans, Etampes and three other tiny towns were under direct royal control in 987 AD.

In Italy the collapse of central authority took an extreme and, until the 19th century, permanent form. Almost surrounded by sea and with potential enemies on all sides, Italy was also torn from within by rival contenders for power. Many sought to buy support by offering immunity from military service to their vassals. Even Otto the Great of Germany's

Book of Maccabees **from St. Gall, c. 924 AD. These warriors are typical of the late Carolingian and early Ottonian eras. (Cod. Periz. F.17, f.22r, University Lib., Leiden)**

29

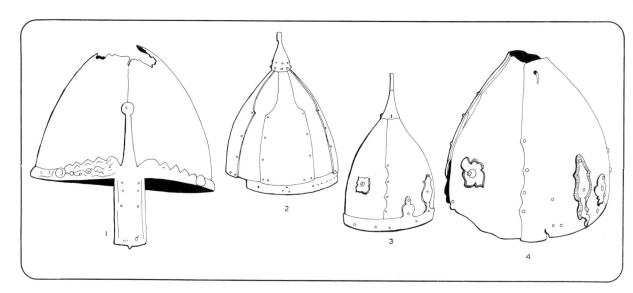

Helmets in the western and eastern traditions: *1* So-called 'Helmet of St. Wenceslas', probably German, 10–11 cent. (Cathedral Treasury, Prague); *2* Western Turkish from Legerevskie, 9–10 cent., southern Ural Mts.; *3–4* So-called Great Polish style of helmet (plus reconstruction), c. 1000 AD (Archaeological Museum, Poznan).

conquest of northern Italy in 962 AD merely slowed this disintegration. Lombardic laws of inheritance led to estates being constantly subdivided. This even affected strategically vital 'marches' until, by the end of the 10th century, the term had lost any real meaning and almost every nobleman now called himself a marquis.

The old 'march levies' had failed against both Saracens and Magyars. Support from the Carolingian kings had rarely been forthcoming, even when Rome itself was threatened, and so the Italians were forced to turn to Byzantium for outside help. Generally, however, they looked after themselves. Byzantine military influence had been dominant in southern Italy for centuries, but even here defence now increasingly fell to local urban militias similar to those which were arising throughout the country.

The second half of the 10th century also saw the *incastellamento* of Italy, a huge growth not only of city walls but also of fortified villages and small castles. In some ways this mirrored the fortification of Germany's eastern frontier, but it was far more spontaneous. The Italian aristocracy was by now very urbanised and contributed an effective cavalry element to the city militias. All free citizens did military service, either as *milites* holding land inside or outside the walls, or as simple *cives* citizens. Militias could be further divided along class lines,

with the rich *optimates militiae* presumably being better equipped than their neighbours.

The church played a primary role in financing fortifications, but the aristocracy, groups of citizens and even individuals were also granted charters permitting them to build defences. Most Italian towns were now, in fact, dependent upon the church rather than upon a feudal aristocracy. Many cities lay under the direct authority of bishops, who soon had their own military followings of *primi milites* or *milites majores*, 'attorneys', *vidame* lieutenants, 'captains of the people', 'captains of the gates', *milites minores* or *secundi milites*, *vavassores* and, at the bottom of this military hierarchy, the *vavassini*. Outside the towns the Italian countryside was to varying degrees feudalised depending on the locality. The descendants of Lombard *gastaldii* and Carolingian counts now enjoyed almost complete autonomy, and the peasantry provided them with an infantry levy of *pedites*, *homines* or *habitatores*. A castle *rocca* or *castello* would be defended by *milites* who held fiefs in the vicinity, although in the Lombard deep south many such castles were garrisoned by mercenaries of humble origins.

Northern Italy, particularly the far north-east, could not escape being drawn into German politics. The Ottonian Emperors constantly tried to impose their control south of the Alps, frequently leading armies across the Brenner or, more rarely, Gothard and Mont Cenis passes. On the other hand many Italian cities, particularly those on the coasts, maintained close links with the Islamic world. Some of the old alliances continued well into the 10th century, Amalfi probably even contributing a fleet to help the Tunisian Fatimid dynasty conquer Egypt. Thereafter the Amalfitan connection remained vital to the Fatimids as a source of wood for ship-building, iron and completed weapons. Most such links were, however, strictly commercial by the 10th century. Business partnerships between Christians, Muslims and Jews were commonplace and the Mediterranean was essentially an unrestricted free-trade area, particularly on the Islamic side. In southern Italy Frankish Carolingian influence had only been a minor element in an extraordinarily mixed military tradition that also included Byzantines, Arabs who had converted to Christianity, Greeks who had turned to Islam, Lombards and native Italians. There is even evidence to suggest that the couched style of using a heavy cavalry lance, soon to be regarded as a typically European knightly manner of fighting, came to the West through this area, having been invented by the Byzantine heavy cavalry of the Emperor Nicephorus Phocas. Elsewhere it is clear that the Italian nobility had adopted Carolingian forms of equipment by the late 9th century.

Cavalry dominated warfare in Italy, as in France and Germany, but the northern cities were also beginning to demonstrate what a trained infantry force could do if equipped with weapons capable of competing effectively with mailed horsemen. In Italy this new infantry weapon was again the pike which, if held by men whose civic discipline enabled them to maintain close-packed ranks, was soon to humble the chivalry both of Italy and Germany. Italian archery was already highly regarded, though there is no evidence of crossbows yet being used in war. It is worth noting that Italian yew wood was exceptionally fine. Most early crossbow laths were probably made of yew, as were both English and Italian longbows.

The *donjon* of Doué-la-Fontaine. The stone hall was converted into a castle around 950 AD by having an upper storey added. (Photo M. de Bouard)

Arms, Armour and Fortification 950-1000 AD

The second half of the 10th century saw rapid economic expansion in western Europe. Iron-working formed part of this development and, though many areas continued to make weapons for local use, a broad swathe of territory from the Rhineland through the Moselle, Meuse and Champagne areas to Berry in central France became the arms-producing heartland of Europe. Other important regions included Catalonia, Norway, the Baltic coast of Germany (which was then Slav Obodrite territory), Tyrol, Styria, Lombardy, Lombardic-Byzantine southern Italy, Saxony, Bohemia and parts of Hungary.

Despite this expansion there is no evidence for improved furnace or forging techniques. Swords were still made by the 'piled' or 'laminated' method, though their shape became less massive, more tapering and suitable for a fencing style of sword-play. Viking influence may have accounted for the popularity of war-axes, usually as an infantry weapon, although Oriental influence might also be seen in the lighter cavalry axes of the western Slavs. The *spangenhelm* was still the most common form of helmet, though conical helms beaten from a single piece of iron were increasingly used. Few changes were seen in armour, though mail hauberks were clearly far more common now than those of scale construction. Some form of absorbent garment was surely worn beneath such hauberks, though padded, quilted coats of Byzantine or Islamic origin probably did not reach most of Europe until the late 11th or 12th century.

One very important weapon which did appear in siege warfare, first being mentioned at Senlis in 947 AD, was the crossbow; yet it remained relatively rare until the 12th century. Crossbows were still of wooden construction and lacked a loading stirrup. The history of the portable crossbow from late Roman times to the 10th century is a mystery. The Byzantine *solenarion* was probably a crossbow, but could have been a bow with a removable arrow-guide of eastern Islamic inspiration. On the other hand crossbows do appear in 10th-century Islamic sources from the Mediterranean region. It would

therefore seem likely that this device remained in use, largely as a hunting weapon, in various areas retaining strong remnants of Roman culture.

Stirrups had now generally been adopted in western Europe and were normally of wrought iron construction. Stirrups alone did not, of course, account for the dominance of cavalry. They did, however, permit both the use of the couched lance and, just as importantly, more effective blows with a long sword, cavalry axe or mace. Most such improvements to European horse harness were of Asiatic origin, including stirrups, chest and crupper straps and nailed horse-shoes. These latter ap-

Arms and armour in manuscripts: *1 Avatea*, **10 cent., south Italian (Ms.3, f.186, Monte Cassino Lib.);** *2 Exultet Roll* **from San Vicenzo al Volturno, 981-7 AD, south Italian (Ms. Lat. 9820, Vatican Lib., Rome);** *3-4 Fulda Sacramentary*, **10 cent., German (Niedersächsische Staats- und Universitätbib., Gottingen);** *5 Beatus* **from Tavera, 975 AD, Mozarab north Spanish (Cathedral Museum, Gerona).**

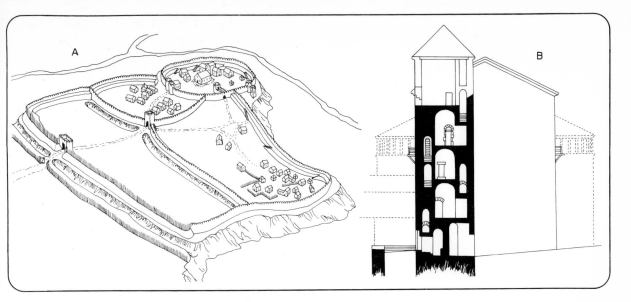

Ottonian fortifications: *A* **Reconstruction of the fortress at Werla, Germany, c. 950 AD (after W. Anderson);** *B* **Section through the square Grannus Tower which was the only defensible part of the Carolingian Palace at Aachen. It was, however, probably built in the very late Carolingian or Ottonian periods (after L. Hugot).**

peared in Germany around 900 AD, and contributed to the endurance of heavy cavalry horses.

Western Europe's growing economic power and its abundant armoury was reflected not only in Slav eastern Europe but also in Byzantium and the entire Islamic world. Even as far as Turkestan and Central Asia Muslims admired 'Frankish' weaponry and imported it in substantial quantities.

Advances in the art of fortification were more dramatic. Castles were naturally numerous in exposed regions such as the Danish, Slav and Hungarian frontiers. Here they formed a network of *burgwards*, a term that also referred to the area dominated by one castle. Such 10th-century fortifications were normally from three to five hectares in area. Their highest concentration was in Flanders and northern France, regions still exposed to Viking attack. Some, including Ghent and Antwerp, began as converted Norse encampments, but more often they had first been built as wooden refuges against the Vikings. In northern Europe most stone defences were built by the Church, though in the south, in Roussillon and Italy, the secular aristocracy also built in expensive stone.

Among the defences ordered by the Emperor Henry of Germany, and continued by his Ottonian successors, were fortified churches. That at Königshof Bodfeld in the Harz Mountains consisted of a church plus a curtain-wall with ditch and towers. Palace-castles like those at Quedlinburg, Pöhlde, Nordhausen, Grone and Duderstadt were now properly fortified, unlike their Carolingian prede-

cessors. Walled abbeys and towns seem to have arisen under the Ottos rather than Henry himself, whereas round *wallburg* ramparts and ditches of ultimately Saxon origin continued to be built even in the 10th century.

The art of fortification was naturally more advanced in Italy. Here a greater variety of terms and defensive devices could be found, including *bertisci* elevated wooden platforms, *meruli* arrow-slits, *propugnacula* wall-towers, *fossato* ditches, *aggeri* or *spizatae* artificial earthen mounds and *turri* turrets. Many walled cities now had a large central tower as the focal point of their defences; but the countryside was also filled with examples of the isolated towers, *castrum* or *castellum*, generally on naturally defensible sites.

It was in France that the most important developments were taking place however. The first was the *motte* and *bailey* castle. Though these are popularly associated with the 11th-century Normans, such defences were widespread by the year 1000 AD. They normally consisted of a wooden turret either on a natural hillock or a man-made *motte*, surrounded by a moated stockade or *bailey*. Even more significant was the appearance of stone *donjons*. Until recently the earliest such large stone keep was thought to be at Langeais. This was built by Fulk Nerra, Count of Anjou, in 994 AD. Recently, however, excavations at nearby Doué-la-Fontaine show that an unfortified stone hall built by the rival Counts of Blois around 900 AD was converted into a true *donjon* some 50 years later. The first Norman *donjons* dated from the close of the century, while *donjons* did not appear in Flanders until some years later. The significance of a *donjon* was that an aristocratic family lived in it all the time. It was not a place of final refuge like the stone towers of Germany or Italy. As with so much in late Carolingian Europe, the *donjon* was a portent of what was to come in the typically 'feudal' age of the 11th and 12th centuries.

When Doué-la-Fontaine was turned into a castle its original ground-floor entrances were blocked up to be replaced by a door directly into the upper storey. (Photo M. de Bouard)

The Plates

A1: Gascon light cavalryman, c. AD 750
Gascons and Basques fought with javelins as light cavalry or light infantry; their tactics had changed little since Roman times. South-western France was, in fact, barely influenced by barbarian Germanic military styles and remained a thoroughly Romanised region. Like all Western European horsemen of the period, Gascons made no use of stirrups, and their saddles were simple padded leather squabs without wooden frames. This warrior's dagger is of an old-fashioned Hispano-Visigothic form. Sources: *Apocalypse*, 8th–9th C. (Cod.31, Stadtbib., Trier); ivory 'Buckle of St. Caesarius', 6th C. (St. Trophime, Arles); carved transenna, 9th C. (*in situ* S. Giovanni Maggiore, Naples).

A2: *Austrasian* scara *mounted infantryman, second half 8th century*

The Austrasians from the north-east of the Frankish state were the basis of Carolingian strength both politically and militarily. This man is a member of an élite *scara* unit under the ruler's direct command; such soldiers still generally fought on foot as mounted infantry, and had relatively heavy armour for the period. Sources: *Sedulius Carmen Pascale*, c. AD 814 (Ms.176, Plant.Mor.Museum, Antwerp); ivory book cover of *Lorsch Gospels*, 9th C. (Vatican Library, Rome); *Apocalypse*, 8th–9th C. (Cod.31, Stadtbib., Trier); 7th C. Frankish sword hilt (Bildarchiv der Stadt Krefeld); 7th–8th C. Lombardic spearhead (Museum of the Early Middle Ages, Rome).

A3: *Lombard cavalryman, mid-8th century*

The Lombards had one of the best-equipped armies in western Europe, and a higher proportion fought as cavalry than in other post-Roman Germanic states. Lombardic equipment was also strongly influenced by militarily more sophisticated neighbours: this man's helmet and lamellar cuirass appear Byzantine, while his belt pendants and short sword show Avar influence. Sources: 'Isola Rizza Dish', 7th C. Lombardic or Italo-Byzantine (Castel Vecchio Museum, Verona); helmet brow-plate, 7th C. Lombardic or Italo-Byzantine (Bargello, Florence); armour, weapons, harness and belt fragments from Nocera Umbra and Castel Trosino, 7th–8th C. (Castel Vecchio Museum, Verona; Bargello, Florence; and Museum of the Early Middle Ages, Rome); Lombard carving, 8th–9th C. (*in situ* Cathedral, Civita Castellana).

B1: *Carolingian* scola *heavy cavalryman, early 9th century*

This cavalryman illustrates many of the problems associated with Carolingian armour. Many manuscripts seem to show scale armour, but none has been found by archaeologists. His helmet is of a type also seen in manuscripts, which might be either an artistic convention, or a transitional form between the late Roman *cassis* and 11th-century southern French two-piece helmets. The élite *scola* were heavily armoured in the latest styles, and their equipment may well have been influenced by the Byzantine and Muslim Arab scale hauberks of the period. A spear resembling that carried by G2

would be carried in battle. Sources: *Stuttgart Psalter*, AD 820–830 (Cod.23, Landesbib., Wurttemberg); 'Donor' fresco, early 9th C. (*in situ* S. Benedetto, Malles); 9th C. French gospel (Ms. 18, Bib. Munic., Amiens); 4th–7th C. Romano-Byzantine helmets (Vojvodjanski Museum, Novi Sad, and Castle Museum, Kerak).

B2: *Armorican cavalryman, mid-9th century*

The problems posed by the Breton equipment are different. Written descriptions exist, but specifically Breton pictorial sources do not. We know, however, that the Bretons were armoured horsemen who fought with javelins in a manner probably inherited from the Alan auxiliaries who settled in Armorica late in the Roman period. There is even mention of horse-armour, probably in the late Roman *clibanarius* style. Sources: 4th–7th C. Romano-Byzantine helmets (Vojvodjanski and Castle Museums, Novi Sad and Kerak); 'Arch of Galerius', early 4th C. (*in situ* Thessaloniki); *Bible of S. Callisto*, 9th C. (S. Paolo fuori le Mura, Rome); 3rd C. Roman horse-armour from Dura Europos (Yale Univ. Art Gallery, New Haven; and Nat. Mus., Damascus); Romano-Sarmatian gravestone from Theodosia, Crimea (Hist. Mus., Kiev); *Codex Aureus*, 9th C. (Clm. 14000, Stadtbib., Munich).

B3: *Frankish infantry levy, first half 9th century*

In complete contrast to the *scola*, the local levy of peasants had to provide their own weaponry, such as this man's primitive war-scythe. Sources: *Martyrologium*, 9th C. (Ms. Lat. Reg. 438, Vatican Library, Rome); *Prudentio*, 9th C. French (Ms. 412, Bib. Munic., Valenciennes); *Stuttgart Psalter*, AD 820–830 (Cod. 23, Landesbib., Wurttemberg).

C1: *Avar aristocratic horseman, late 8th century*

The demands of realism, clarity and artistic composition have defeated us here: the plate is unrealistic in that C1 must be the defeated enemy of C2 and C3 in a scene such as this!

The Avars who conquered present-day Hungary had a profound influence on their Byzantine and (to a lesser extent) Frankish neighbours. They introduced much new military technology, including the early man-powered mangonel (see background) from China; the Central Asian stirrup; the framed saddle, and lighter forms of horse-armour.

This man carries a silk 'wind-sock' type of banner, and holds a straight sword whose guard is cut from a solid agate. His heavy felt coat, of Turkestani cut, is silk-lined and has applied silk decoration at the edges and on the upper arms. Note the 'gaiters', which have a narrow section passing up the front of the knee and tied round the leg above it; and the pigtails just visible below the helmet aventail. The belt pendants are typically Central Asian.

His horse has a stiff leather chamfron; multi-layered felt armour covers its neck and forequarters only, partly covered by a Chinese cloth thrown over the saddle, which is relatively high-framed; the tail is plaited, and the crupper and chamfron straps are decorated with small bells. Typically, a hand-axe with a very narrow blade parallel to the haft (on a 'stalk') might hang from the saddle. The accompanying line drawing illustrates the stirrup.

Sources: 7th–8th C. Avar horse furniture and belt fragments (Nat. Mus., Budapest); 5th–7th C. Avar sword fragments and helmets from the Crimea and southern Urals (Hermitage, Leningrad); 6th–8th C. frescoes (in situ Varaksha, Kumtara and Kizil; and from Kizil in Staatliche Mus., West Berlin).

C2: Western Slav tribesman, c. AD 800
The Slav tribes who paid tribute to the Carolingians also provided auxiliary troops. This man has the front of his head shaved in pagan Slav fashion,

Left: **A possible reconstruction of a simple leather strap/ wooden peg stirrup, of a kind we may perhaps associate with Plate D3. The 9th-century Spanish or Carolingian** *Apocalypse* **Ms, now at Valenciennes, shows a variety of riders, some using simple stirrups and some without.** *Centre and right*: **Cast iron stirrup from Hungary, which we may perhaps associate with the Avar, Plate C2. This type, with an up-curved step, seems to have been in use for a long period and over much of Europe. Representations of simple metal stirrups are found in T'ang artefacts in Turkestan from at least the late 7th century. (Drawings by Richard Hook)**

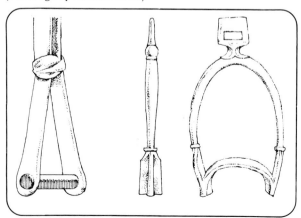

though the whole scalp may also have been shaved. He carries a narrow-bladed axe typical of this region; and wears short, loose trousers tied above the knee. Sources: Gravestone from Magdeburg area, c. AD 700 (Landesmus., Halle); 8th–9th C. Moravian weapons (Regional Museums, Brno, Mikulčice and Martin).

C3: Saxon infantry levy, c. AD 800
The simple longbow seems to have survived longer in Saxony and Denmark than in many other parts of Continental Europe. Some examples were more than man-high. This levy is rather well-armed for a peasant; he has a traditional German *seax*, and an imported Moravian sword. Sources: 7th C. gravestone from Hornhausen (Landesmus., Bonn); 8th C. Moravian sword (Regional Mus., Nitra); 5th C. Danish bow from Nydam.

D1: The Emperor Charlemagne, with Imperial banner; early 9th century
Einhard wrote of Charlemagne that 'only very rarely and only in Rome did he dress in the Roman [i.e. Byzantine] fashion'. Here the Emperor displays a banner that was probably given him by Pope Leo III. Sources: 9th C. mosaic (in situ S. Giovanni in Laterano, Rome); *Bible of S. Callisto*, 9th C. (S. Paolo fuori le Mura, Rome); 9th C. sword from the Seine (private collection); 9th C. statue of Charlemagne (in situ St. John's Church, Müstair).

D2: Papal guardsman, early 9th century
This soldier's highly decorated equipment reminds us that Byzantine fashion dominated in Rome. His tunic is also adorned with an imported Islamic *tiraz* or embroidered band of material, probably from Egypt. Sources: Mid-8th C. fresco (in situ S. Maria Antiqua, Rome); 9th C. Byzantine psalter (Ms. 61, Monastery of the Pantocrator, Mt. Athos); 7th–8th C. shield boss from Nocera Umbra (Museum of the Early Middle Ages, Rome); 'Donor' fresco, early 9th C. (in situ S. Benedetto, Malles).

D3: Mounted infantryman, Spanish March; early 9th century
The warriors of northern Spain were naturally influenced by their Muslim Andalusian neighbours. Some even used the leather 'loop stirrup': an accompanying line drawing illustrates a possible

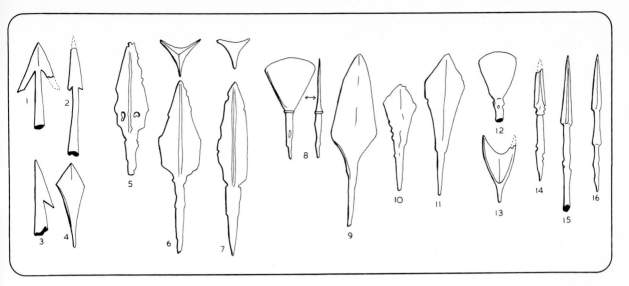

leather and wood stirrup for this man. His fine mail hauberk and iron helmet are probably of Muslim manufacture. His long spear would have been used as a pike. Sources: *Apocalypse*, Spanish (?) c. AD 840 (Ms. 99, Bib. Munic., Valenciennes); *Beatus Commentaries*, Mozarab, c. AD 950 (Ms. 644, Pierpont Morgan Library, NY); fragment of Islamic plate, 10th C. (Madina al Zahra Mus., Cordoba).

E1: Northern French cavalryman, c. AD 900

By the early 10th century most European *miles*, or professional soldiers, had adopted the stirrup and framed saddle. They had yet to acquire the couched style of using a lance; this still had 'wings' or lugs below the blade, probably indicating a thrust-and-parry style of fighting. Mail hauberks slit at the sides rather than the front and back also suggest that this class of soldier were as accustomed to fighting on foot as on horseback. Note iron prick-spurs with gilt decoration, worn over the leather shoes. The strap over the left shoulder might support a horn on the right hip. Horse harness with a knotted effect (for adjustment?) appears in many contemporary sources over a wide range of dates and areas. Sources: *Psalterium Aureum*, c. AD 880 (Cod. 22, Stiftsbib., St. Gall); gospel from Corbie, 9th C. (Ms. 172, Bib. Comm., Amiens); 9th C. French psalter (Ms. 18, Bib. Munic., Amiens); 10th C. Rhenish sword (Ethnog. Mus., Lodz).

E2: French local infantryman, early 10th century

Although cavalry now dominated Western Euro-

Arrowheads: *1–4* **Moravian, 7–8 cent., from Mikulčice, Czechoslovakia;** *5–13* **Avar, 6–8 cent., Hungary;** *14–16* **Magyar, 9–10 cent., from Tuzsér, Hungary.**

pean warfare, infantry still had a role in rough terrain or during sieges. Most were simple peasant levies. Sources: *Ebbo Gospel*, 9th C. (Ms. 1, Bib. Munic., Epernay); *Psychomachia*, 9th–10th C. (Ms. 264, Stadtbib., Bern); *Bible of Charles the Bald* from St. Denis, c. AD 870 (S. Paolo fuori le Mura, Rome); 9th–10th C. Viking spearheads (Hist. Mus., Stockholm, and London Museum).

E3: Carolingian nobleman, late 9th century

The wealth of the Carolingian Empire was concentrated in the hands of the Church, and of an aristocracy which largely failed to rise to the Viking challenge. This man's costume reflects some Byzantine and Islamic fashions; his highly decorated sword is, however, of Scandinavian origin. Sources: *Apocalypse of St. Amand*, 9th C. (Ms. 386, Bib. Munic., Cambrai); *Bible of S. Callisto*, from Corbie, 9th C. (S. Paolo fuori le Mura, Rome); *Bible of Charles the Bald*, 9th C. (Ms. Lat. 1, Bib. Nat., Paris); Carolingian brooch (Nieder Österreich. Landesmus., Vienna); 9th–10th C. Viking sword (Nat. Mus. of Ireland, Dublin).

F1: Italian infantry levy, early 10th century

The cities of Italy never lost their military role, though their militias were often very poorly equipped. This man relies largely on a heavy wooden club, and a cloak wrapped around his arm as a rudimentary shield. Sources: *Avatea*, south

The silver-gilt *Chasse de St. Hadelin* in the church of St. Martin, Vise, dates from 1046 AD but it still shows the earlier style of mail hauberk, which was slit at the sides rather than the front and back. Such armours were primarily designed for fighting on foot. (Photo Collégiale St. Martin, Vise)

Italian, 10th C. (Ms. 3, Monte Cassino); 'Arthurian Cycle' mosaic, 9th–10th C. (*in situ* Church of the Pantocrator, Otranto); 'Crucifixion', south Italian ivory plaque, 10th–11th C. (Kaiser Friedrich Mus., Berlin).

F2: Italian 'gastald' cavalryman, early 10th century
Assailed by both Muslims and Magyars, Italy largely had to rely on its own military resources. The most important were a class of minor aristocrats, many of whom were descended from the Lombard *gastaldii*. This southern Italian *miles* has a slightly curved sword, a kite-shaped shield, and decorative horse collars, all showing Byzantine influence from southern Italy. Sources: 10th C. Exultet Rolls (Ms. Lat. 9820, Vatican Library, Rome, and Ms. 2, John Rylands Library, Manchester); ivory situla from Milan, c. AD 950–1000 (Victoria & Albert Mus., London); 9th C. Byzantine silk fabric (Textile Mus., Lyons).

F3: North African infantry archer, early 10th century
The Berbers and Arabs who raided Italy in the 10th century included both volunteers and professional soldiers. This Berber is one of the latter. His quilted tunic is typically North African, and his composite bow is of the large Arab form. His single-edged sword, without a guard or quillons, is of the type which would develop later into the Moroccan *flysa*. Sources: 10th–11th C. ceramic plaques and plates from Sabra (Bardo, Tunis); Sicilian ivory boxes and oliphants, 11th C. (Staats Mus., West Berlin; Met. Mus., NY; and Victoria & Albert Mus., London); 10th–11th C. Tunisian ceramics (Benaki Mus., Athens).

G1: German infantryman, first half 10th century
German peasant levies, many of Saxon origin, had the simplest of weapons. This man wears a crude basket-weave helmet; his weapons are a knife, and a long, rather angular, flat-section wooden bow. Sources: *Codex Egberti*, from Reichenau, c. AD 980 (Ms. 24, Stadtbib., Trier); flat-bow from Asby, 5th–8th C. (Hist. Mus., Stockholm).

G2: German cavalryman, first half 10th century
The Ottonian emperors built up a large cavalry force to face the Magyar and Viking threats; but their equipment, although relatively heavy, often appears to have been rather crude when compared to that of their southern neighbours. This man wears a simple two-piece iron helmet with a leather aventail or coif, and a short mail hauberk. He is armed only with a spear. This follows a common style in having a leather thong or fabric strip wound spirally down its whole length as a strengthening feature, perhaps picked out in colour; and 'wings' or lugs below the blade. Sources: *Book of Maccabees* from St. Gall, c. AD 925 (Cod. Periz. F.17, University Library, Leiden); *Pericopean Buch*, 10th C. (Ms. 15A, Bisch. Ord. Bib., Augsburg); ivory situla from Trier, late 10th C. (Cathedral Mus., Aachen).

G3: Magyar nobleman, first half 10th century
The way of life of the Magyar warrior aristocracy was similar to that of the Iranian nobility; certainly, their equipment had the same Central Asian origins. This man's segmented *spangenhelm*, sabre and bow are in this tradition. The sabre is gently

curved, and is slung from the left hip beside the case for the unstrung bow—an item long out of fashion in the East. It has a rather angularly curved shape, and is of leather with bone plates at the open end. The double-breasted felt coat is fastened right across under the left arm. He wears Asian-style fur-lined boots without heels, whose legs button down the outside, the exposed edge cut to a decorative shape; and silvered prick-spurs. Sources: 9th–10th C. Magyar grave-goods, weapons and horse harness (Nat. Mus., Budapest); 9th C. Magyar silver bowl from Urals (Hermitage, Leningrad).

H1: Southern French knight, late 10th century

With the growing uniformity of armour and equipment, the *miles* or knight of north and south used almost identical arms and armour: cf. this figure with H2. This knight's coif would be tightened across the chin in battle. He carries an early form of single-edged falchion; this might show Islamic influence, or equally it might be a development of the much earlier *seax*. Sources: 10th–11th C. gospel (Ms. 8, Bib. Munic., Boulogne); *Atlantic Bible*, southern French, 11th C. (Ms. Edili 125–126, Bib. Laur., Florence); *Beatus Commentaries* from Tavera, AD 975 (Cathedral Mus., Gerona); Bible, c. AD 960 (Ms. 2, San Isidoro, Leon).

H2: Lotharangian knight, late 10th century

By this date the Western European *miles* was almost indistinguishable from the men who won the battle of Hastings and marched on the First Crusade. Only the lack of a nasal on this man's conical helmet, and the slits at the sides of his hauberk, are old-fashioned features. His cloak is decorated with Byzantine brocade, and his saddle shows some Eastern European influences. He brandishes the weapons of his Slav prisoner.

H3: Western Slav warrior, second half 10th century

The western Slav tribes and states used equipment similar to that of Western Europe and Scandinavia. Only this man's so-called 'Great Polish' or Russian style of segmented *spangenhelm*, with its mail aventail, betrays oriental influence; though his shield may also be significant. It is deeply convex, made of wickerwork, and has a straight wooden grip right across the open face. Sources: 10th C.

The Boosenburg at Rüdesheim. This stepped tower-fortress overlooking the Rhine probably dates from the 10th century, though it may even be from the 9th.

spearhead from Szezecin; 10th–12th C. axe from Lake Lednicke (Mus. of the First Piasts, Lednica); helmet from Gorzuchy, c. AD 1000 (Archaeol. Mus., Poznan); 11th C. silver bowl from Wloclawek (Archaeol. Mus., Warsaw).

Further Reading

W. Anderson, *Castles of Europe from Charlemagne to the Renaissance* (London, 1970)

B. S. Bachrach, '*Charles Martel, Mounted Shock Combat, the Stirrup and Feudalism*'; *Studies in medieval and Renaissance History* VII (1970), pp. 49–75

J. Beeler, *Warfare in Feudal Europe 730–1200* (Ithaca, 1971)

P. Contamine, *La Guerre au Moyen Âge* (Paris, 1980)

C. Erdmann, '*Die Burgenordnung Heinrichs I*', *Deutsches Archiv für Erforschung des Mittelalters* VI (1943), pp. 59–101

K. Fischer Drew, '*The Carolingian Military Frontier in Italy*', *Traditio* XX (1964), pp. 437–447

F. Heer, *Charlemagne and his World* (London, 1975)

A. R. Lewis, *Naval Power and Trade in the Mediterranean AD 500–1100* (Princeton, 1951)

K. J. Leyser, *Medieval Germany and its Neighbours 900–1250* (London, 1982)

P. Llewellyn, *Rome in the Dark Ages* (London, 1971)

M. Lombard, *Les Métaux dans l'ancien Monde du Ve au XIe siècle* (Paris, 1974)

E. Oakeshott, *The Archaeology of Weapons* (London, 1960)

Ordinamenti Militari in Occidente nell'alto Medioevo: Settimane di Studi del Centro Italiani di Studi sull'alto Medioevo XV/1 (Spoleto, 1968)

D. J. A. Ross, *'L'Originalité de Turoldus: le maniement de la lance'*, *Cahiers de Civilization Medievale* VI (1963), pp. 127–138

J. F. Verbruggen, *'L'art militaire dans l'empire Carolingien'*, *Revue Belge d'Histoire Militaire* XXIII (1979–80), pp. 289–310 and 393–412

J. F. Verbruggen, *The Art of Warfare in Western Europe during the Middle Ages* (Oxford, 1977)

J. F. Verbruggen, *'L'armée et la stratégie de Charlemagne'*, in *Karl der Grosse, vol. I: Persönlichkeit und Geschichte* (Dusseldorf, 1965), pp. 420–436

Notes sur les planches en couleur

A1 Les Gascons et les Basques du sud-est de la France se battirent avec des javelins dans la cavalerie légère et l'infanterie légère; leur équipement et leurs méthodes étaient essentiellement toujours ceux de l'époque romaine. **A2** Ces fantassins montés, revêtus d'armures relativement lourdes pour leur époque, constituaient la base de la force carolingienne. Les unités 'scara' étaient sous la commande directe de l'empereur. **A3** Les Lombards possédaient les forces les mieux équipées de l'Europe occidentale et une plus grande proportion de cavalerie que d'autres armées. L'armure présentait une certaine influence byzantine et avar.

B1 Les unités 'scola', aux lourdes armures, posent des problèmes aux historiens. Les manuscripts les montrent revêtus d'armures de ce type; mais l'archéologie n'a pas produit d'exemples du casque ou de l'armure en écailles. **B2** Les textes descriptifs semblent indiquer que les troupes auxiliaires Alan se sont établies en Armorique vers la fin de l'époque romaine, et cette illustration est inspirée de telles descriptions. **B3** Les paysans recrutés fournissaient leur propre équipement rudimentaire, dont cette faux de guerre est un exemple.

C1 Notez l'aspect oriental de ce cavalier de la Hongrie d'aujourd'hui. Ces cavaliers experts, qui utilisaient des étriers en fer, eurent une grande influence tant sur les Byzantins que sur les Francs. L'armure en toile du cheval ne couvre que le cou et les quartiers de devant. **C2** Notez le front rasé caratéristique et la hache typique à lame étroite. **C3** Plutôt mieux armé que la plupart des paysans recrutés, ce Saxon a un arc, un 'seax' allemand et une épée moravienne.

D1 L'empereur porte la bannière qui lui a probablement été donnée par le pape Léon III. **D2** L'influence byzantine à Rome explique le costume très décoré de cet homme, qui possède même des caractéristiques islamiques. **D3** L'influence musulmane se faisait fortement sentir à la frontière espagnole et ce fantassin monté a un casque et une cotte de mailles qui sont probablement de fabrication musulmane. Des étriers en 'boucle' simple peuvent avoir éfe utilisés.

E1 A cette date, la plupart des soldats professionnels utilisaient des étriers et des selles à cadre élevé; mais la lance était probablement encore utilisée pour des coups de botte et de parade plutôt que pour être ancrée sous le bras durant la charge. **E2** Les levées d'infanterie composées de simples paysans avaient encore un rôle à jouer durant les sièges ou les batailles sur terrains difficiles. **E3** La mode byzantine et islamique ainsi qu'une épée de style scandinave sont en évidence dans cette illustration.

F1 Ce paysan recruté par levée ne dispose pour se protéger que d'une massue en boie et de son manteau enroulé autour du bras. **F2** Des petits aristocrates, descendants des 'gastaldii' lombards, ont joué un rôle important dans la défense de l'Italie contre de nombreux ennemis; l'épée légèrement courbée et le bouclier en forme de cerf-volant sont deux signes de l'influence byzantine. **F3** Soldat professionnel, avec armure capitonnée typique d'Afrique du nord.

G1 Le 'casque' est en vannerie tressée; les armes sont limitées à leur plus simple expression: un arc et un couteau. **G2** Quoique lourdement équipée, la cavalerie allemande de l'époque des empereurs ottomans portait une armure plutôt primitive en comparaison avec les styles du sud. **G3** Des caractéristiques typiques de l'Asie Centrale sont en évidence dans le costume de cet aristocrate magyar, au long manteau de feutre, portant un sabre et un arc sur la hanche droite.

H1, H2 L'armure des 'chevaliers' de l'Europe occidentale et de l'Europe méridionale était à cette époque presque identique, avec seulement des variations mineures de style. **H3** Ce prisonnier slave porte une armure similaire à celle de ses vainqueurs, seul le 'spangenhelm' appelé 'grand polonais' témoignant de l'influence de l'Orient.

Farbtafeln

A1 In der leichten Infanterie und in der leichten Kavallerie kämpften die Gaskonen und Basken aus dem Südwesten Frankreichs mit Speeren. Ihre Ausrüstung und ihre Methoden waren im Grunde noch genau so wie zu römischen Zeiten. **A2** Diese für ihre Zeit relativ schwer bewaffneten, berittenen Infanteristen bildeten die Stärke der Karolinger. Die *Scara*-Einheiten unterstanden dem Herrscher direkt. **A3** Die Langobarden hatten die am besten ausgerüstete Armee in Westeuropa, und ihre Kavallerie war grösser als die anderer Streitkräfte. Die Waffen lassen auf byzantinischen und awarischen Einfluss schliessen.

B1 Die schwer bewaffneten *Scola*-Einheiten bereiten den Historikern Probleme. Manuskripten gemäss waren sie so bewaffnet, wie hier gezeigt, aber es gibt keinerlei archäologischen Beweis für den Helm und die Plattenrüstung. **B2** Schriftlichen Überlieferungen zufolge liessen sich alanische Hilfstruppen zur spätrömischen Zeit in Armorica nieder. Dieses Gemälde beruht auf derartigen Überlieferungen. **B3** Bauerntruppen stellten ihre Ausrüstung selbst, wie zum Beispiel diese Sense.

C1 Achten Sie auf den orientalischen Einfluss bei diesem Reiter aus dem heutigen Ungarn. Diese fortgeschrittenen Kavalleristen verwendeten eiserne Steigbügel und hatten beträchtlichen Einfluss auf Byzantiner und Franken. Die Pferderüstung aus Stoff bedeckt lediglich den Hals und die Kruppe. **C2** Charakteristisch sind hier der Haarschnitt an der Stirne sowie seine typische, schmale Axt. **C3** Dieser Sachse ist besser bewaffnet als die meisten Bauerntruppen: er trägt einen Bogen, ein germanisches *Seax* sowie ein mährisches Schwert.

D1 Der Kaiser trägt eine Fahne, die ihm wahrscheinlich Papst Leo III gegeben hat. **D2** Die verzierte Uniform dieses Mannes beweist den byzantinischen Einfluss in Rom; hier sind sogar islamische Merkmale erkennbar. **D3** An der spanischen Grenze war der moslemische Einfluss sehr stark. Der Helm und das Kettenhemd dieses berittenen Infanteristen sind wahrscheinlich moslemischer Herkunft. Damals wurden einfache, schlauferförmige Steigbügel verwendet.

E1 Zu dieser Zeit verwendeten die meisten Berufssoldaten Steigbügel und Sattel mit hohen Rahmen; die Lanze diente wahrscheinlich zum Abwurf bzw. zur Abwehr. Man hielt sie damals noch nicht angriffsbereit unter dem Arm. **E2** Einfache Bauerntruppen spielten bei Belagerungen und bei Kämpfen in rauhen Gegenden immer noch eine Rolle. **E3** Diese Figur weist auf byzantinische und islamische Mode hin und trägt ein skandinavisches Schwert.

F1 Dieser Bauernsoldat trägt weiter nichts als einen Holzknüppel; sein um den Arm geschlungener Mantel dient als Schild. **F2** Der von den langobardischen *Gastaldii* entsprungene Niedrigadel spielte bei der Verteidigung Italiens gegen viele Feinde eine grosse Rolle. Das leicht gekrümmte Schwert und das drachenförmige Schild deuten auf byzantinischen Einfluss hin. **F3** Ein Berufssoldat mit für Nordafrika typischer, gepolsterter Rüstung.

G1 Der 'Helm' besteht aus einem Korbgeflecht; die Waffen bestehen lediglich aus Bogen und Messer. **G2** Zur Zeit der osmanischen Kaiser war die germanische Kavallerie zwar schwer bewaffnet, aber im Vergleich zur Kavallerie aus südlichen Ländern stand sie zurück. **G3** Typisch mittelasiatische Merkmale erkennt man an der Uniform dieses magyarischen Edelmanns, an seinem langen Filzmantel sowie seinem Säbel und Bogen über der linken Hüfte.

H1, H2 Die Ritterrüstungen in Nord- und Südeuropa unterschieden sich mit Ausnahme kleiner Abweichungen zu dieser Zeit kaum. **H3** Der besiegte Slawe trägt eine ähnliche Uniform wie die des Siegers, und nur der 'grosspolnische' *Spangenhelm* lässt auf orientalischen Einfluss schliessen.